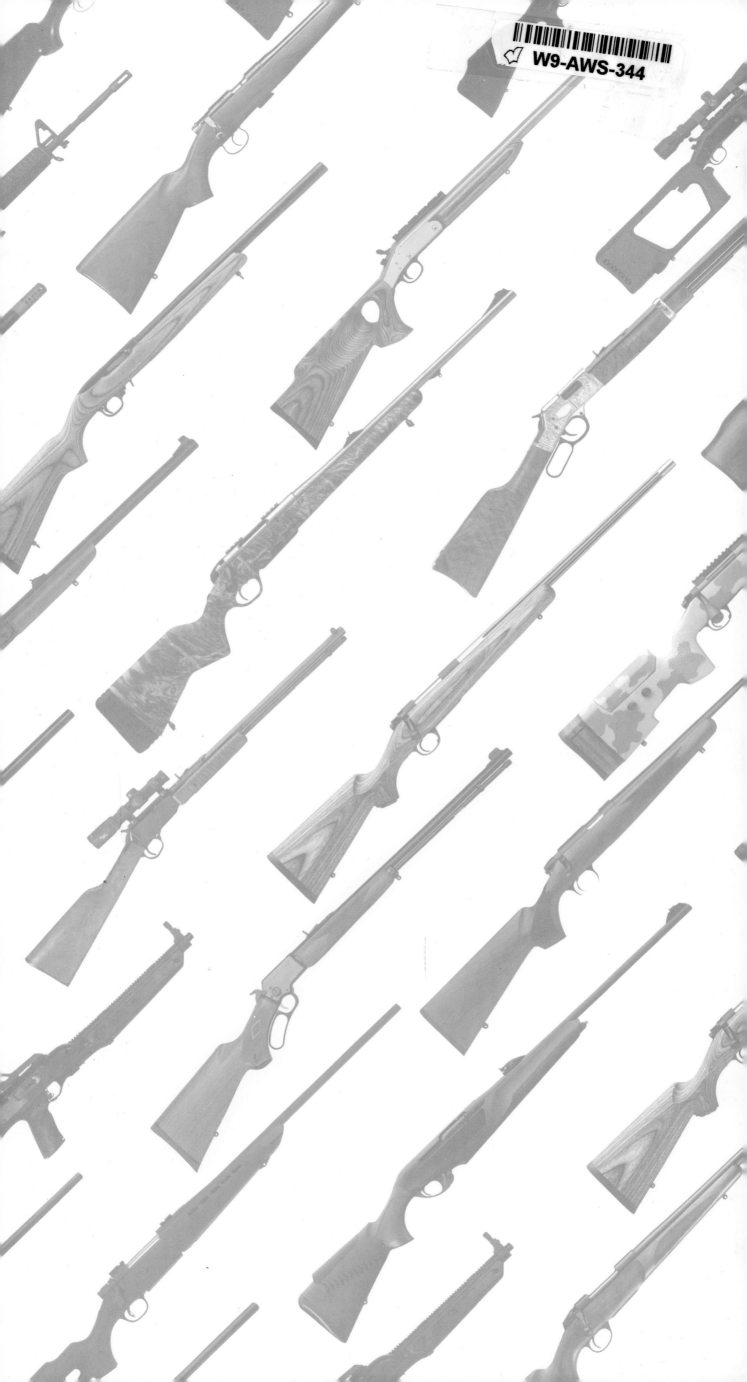

RIFLES

RIFLES

Doug Wicklund & Jim Supica

THUNDER BAY
P·R·E·S·S

San Diego, California

THUNDER BAY
P·R·E·S·S

Thunder Bay Press
An imprint of the Baker & Taylor Publishing Group
10350 Barnes Canyon Road, San Diego, CA 92121
www.thunderbaybooks.com

First Published 2010
Reprinted & Revised 2011, 2012

Produced by TAJ Books International LLP
27, Ferndown Gardens,
Cobham,
Surrey,
UK,
KT11 2BH
www.tajbooks.com

Copyright ©2010 Taj Books International LLP

Company history text supplied by Karen Vellucci

Photos courtesy Jim Supica, ArmchairGunShow.com
pages 6, 8, 10, 11 (bottom), 12 (both), 14

You can join the NRA by contacting them at:

The National Rifle Association of America
11250 Waples Mill Road
Fairfax VA 22030

or by visiting their website, www.nra.org

And you can view the treasures of the NRA National Firearms Museum at the website
www.nramuseum.org.

The museum is open every day of the week, except major holidays, at NRA Headquarters in Fairfax, VA, near
Washington, DC. There is no admission charge.

All notations of errors or omissions should be addressed to Thunder Bay Press, Editorial Department, at the
above address. All other correspondence (author inquiries, permissions) concerning the content of this book
should be addressed to TAJ Books, 27, Ferndown Gardens, Cobham, Surrey, UK, KT11 2BH, info@tajbooks.com.

ISBN-10: 1-60710-095-9
ISBN-13: 978-1-60710-095-9

Library of Congress Cataloging-in-Publication Data available on request
Printed in China.

3 4 5 14 13 12

CONTENTS

Introduction

The classic Kentucky (or Pennsylvania) rifle is one of the earliest uniquely American designs. Distinctive features include long barrel with stock forearm extending to the muzzle, gracefully turned down buttstock, and ornate brass patchbox designs. Makers sometimes signed their names on the barrel.

A Brief History of Rifles

From the earliest days of civilization, weapons have been among man's most important tools. While primarily used to provide for food and protection, firearms have also served to maintain social order, and to defend specific areas of settlement.

Beyond their military applications, many firearms, particularly rifles, have also come to be used for a wide variety of recreational and competitive shooting, and millions of Americans regularly exercise their constitutional right to own firearms simply for the pleasure of shooting, or the enjoyment of ownership.

The first firearms, ca. 1350, called "hand cannons" or "hand gonnes" were essentially small cannons designed to be held or attached to a pole for use by individual soldiers. Loaded and fired in the same manner as full-sized cannons, these portable arms were viewed by clergy of the day as being diabolical in nature, and users had to undergo a special religious ceremony to avoid spiritual contamination.

For the next four centuries, the greatest advances in the evolution of firearms would focus primarily on the search for more reliable methods of igniting the gunpowder, in addition to design advances for more rapid repeat shots and better accuracy. The advent of rifling serves as the dividing point between rifled arms (rifles) and unrifled arms (smoothbores).

The term "lock, stock and barrel" comes from firearms design, representing the three major components of early guns. The barrel is self-explanatory, and the stock is, of course, the wooden holder in which the barrel is mounted to allow the gun to be fired from the shoulder or from one hand. The lock is the mechanical contrivance that is used to ignite the charge of gunpowder held in the chamber of the barrel.

The first gun to combine these three components was the matchlock, developed in the early 1400s. A holder for the burning match, called a serpentine, allowed the flame source to be brought to the touchhole. This simple system was followed by a much more complicated one, the wheel lock in the early 1500s. This ignition system is similar to a modern cigarette lighter.

While an improvement in reliability over the matchlock, as the smoldering slow match no longer required constant attention, it took highly skilled craftsmen to build the clocklike mechanism of the wheel lock, making it an extremely expensive piece, primarily available to royalty and the noble class for hunting. Although wheel locks saw some military use, the matchlock remained the most common military firearm during the wheel lock era.

Improvements using flint against steel to provide the igniting spark continued in the second half of the sixteenth century, with two early examples being the snaphance, the first flintlock type gun ca. 1560, and the miquelet, following a couple decades later.

The snaphance held a piece of flint in the hammer/cock, with a pan of priming powder mounted on the outside of the barrel over the touchhole as with the matchlock system. Pulling the trigger would release the cock to swing rapidly forward striking the battery, and showering sparks into the pan, hopefully firing the gun.

Around 1580, the miquelet system provided an improvement to the snaphance by combining the battery and pan cover into a single piece, called the frizzen. This L-shaped spring-loaded piece would pivot to cover the pan after priming with powder. When the cock was released, it would swing forward striking the frizzen, producing sparks while pushing the frizzen up and forward to expose the powder in the pan to the sparks.

In the early 1600s, the basic design of the flintlock, or French lock, was perfected. The flintlock moved components from the outside of the lockplate, where they were exposed to elements and damage, to the interior of the lock.

Improvements in Accuracy

As flintlock systems were developed, two improvements were introduced that dramatically increased the accuracy of firearms. Archers discovered if the feathers on their arrows were angled, causing the arrow to rotate in flight, their ability to hit the target was improved. This concept was applied to guns by cutting slowly twisting grooves down the interior length of the barrel, imparting spin to the bullet as it left the muzzle. These grooves were called rifling, and "rifled muskets" or "rifles" so equipped were found to be much better at hitting their mark over further distances than smoothbore muskets. With the improved accuracy possible with rifled firearms, a system of aiming other than pointing became more important, and early sights came into use. A common system was a notch of some type at the rear of the barrel and a post on the front. With this open sight, the top of the front sight post is aligned with the target, and the post is centered within the rear sight notch, with the top of the post level within the notch. When correctly aligned with the bore axis, these basic sights provide accuracy for short-range shooting needs.

Early Rifles in America

Despite pictures of Pilgrims with blunderbusses, early firearms in America were usually matchlocks and the occasional wheel lock. Firearms were expensive commodities in Europe, with individuals with military experience later owning arms in civilian private life. However, during the Colonial years, a distinctly American arm would be developed, by hundreds of gunsmiths emerging throughout the new land. In the 1600s and 1700s, colonists coming to America brought their European firearms and design concepts with them. Any gun was a necessary and treasured tool when pioneering the frontier wilderness, and individual gunmakers who had started off as blacksmiths or jewelers, were valued and essential members of the small settlements.

The American long rifle, better known as the Kentucky or Pennsylvania rifle, was derived from the German Jaeger (translated "hunter") type flintlock, a practical European rifle well suited for hunting game at close quarters in the dark forests of the Old World. In the New World, this rifle slowly evolved into a longer arm with a full-length wooden stock, while the rear of the buttstock developed a graceful curve, culminating in a shoulder-contoured buttplate. Embellished versions would come to be decorated with brass or silver inlays in the stock. Wood and, later, brass patchbox covers in the stock became more elaborate and decorative. Many of these designs became proprietary to specific gunsmiths or localities. The Kentucky rifle became the household gun/ tool that fed and defended early pioneer families. Marksmanship was a valued, necessary, and common skill regularly practiced. Community "beef shoots" set local marksmen against their peers in contests that rewarded excellence with meat, and for the lowest scorer, the wooden target stop with all the fired lead as an incentive to improve their skills.

Military doctrine of the time called for the massed use of smoothbores as the primary martial firearm. Although less accurate than rifled arms, smoothbores allowed faster reloading, since a lead ball slightly smaller than bore diameter could be quickly rammed down the barrel with wadding, even as the barrel became fouled from gunpowder residue from previous shots. The patched lead bullet for a rifled arm must fit the bore tightly to engage the rifling, and takes more time and effort to ram home. The powder charge for

A selection of classic rifles on display at a gun show.

The American Civil War was a time of rapid evolution in firearms design. Shown here are a Colt 1851 Navy Revolver and Spencer repeating carbine, both used by Captain William Weston of the 7th Kansas Volunteers.

the rifle is usually a precisely measured charge of finer-grained powder, while the musket received a generic dose of cruder powder, measured by approximate volume.

The established European rules were changing, however, and in the French and Indian War, the Revolutionary War, and the War of 1812, American marksmen used their rifles and well-honed shooting skills on selected targets from longer distances and from behind cover. Choosing significant targets to engage, like officers and artillerymen, made American sharpshooters a force to contend with in the Colonial

era. After securing independence, the new country rapidly sought its own means of mass-producing military arms, establishing two national government arsenals for the manufacture of firearms at Springfield, Massachusetts, in 1795 and Harpers Ferry, Virginia, in 1800. These two national armories first produced smoothbore muskets, still a useful military arm. However, the age of the rifle as an essential marksman's weapon had arrived.

In addition to arsenal-made firearms, the United States' government and some states contracted with small gunmakers to produce military weapons or parts based on sample patterns provided by the government. America's oldest continuing gunmaker traces its lineage to this era, with Eliphalet Remington producing barrels as early as 1826. The Remington firm remains one of America's premier gun manufacturers today. The famous Henry Deringer, whose name later would become synonymous with small concealable handguns, produced flintlock rifles for the United States' government as early as 1810; as did Eli Whitney's Whitney Arms nearly a decade earlier. Small gunsmiths that had produced Kentucky rifles, now offered slightly altered pieces to meet contract rifle specifications in 1792 and trade arms needed for western expansion.

The Percussion System

Although flintlocks lingered for nearly two centuries, problems remained. Shooters usually had to carry two types of powder–fine for priming and coarse for the main charge, and this ignition system was unreliable in wet weather. It was difficult to store a flintlock gun loaded and ready for immediate use over any extended period. In 1807 a Scottish clergyman, Reverend Alexander Forsyth, is credited with developing an ignition system based on the principle that certain unstable chemical fulminates detonate when struck a sharp blow, a concept still used in toy cap pistols and fireworks today.

Various methods to utilize this explosive approach were tried, and in 1814 the percussion cap was perfected by Joshua Shaw. The percussion cap is a cuplike holder of mercury fulminate that can be quickly pressed onto a nipple mounted in the rear of a gun barrel. When the trigger is pulled, the hammer strikes the cap, beginning the explosion that sparks through a hole in the nipple into the main charge in the barrel, firing the gun. Percussion ignition offered such obvious advantages to the flintlock method that most gunmakers adapted their existing designs to percussion ignition, although within 50 years, it too would be obsolete.

Repeaters and Breechloaders

The advent of percussion ignition marked the beginning of rapid firearms' advancements, coinciding with the Industrial Revolution, the American Civil War, and the turn of the century. During this relatively brief time, guns would go from primitive muzzle-loading flintlocks to the breech-loading systems that still dominate firearms designs today.

From the matchlock to the early percussion era, the vast majority of guns had been muzzleloaders. Both powder and projectile had to be loaded at the muzzle and rammed to the rear before firing. Reloading was awkward, especially if trying to shoot a longarm from a prone position or behind cover or concealment, and the job became more difficult after a few shots when barrel fouling made the job more strenuous. The best of these breechloaders was patented in 1776 by Patrick Ferguson and utilized a screw-threaded breechlock that rotated down to expose an opening into the barrel. This led to many attempts to develop a gun that loaded from the rear of the barrel, although most early efforts were not effective due to weakness of materials and leakage of hot gases from the breech seal when the gun was fired.

In the early nineteenth century, various breechloading designs finally reached production in quantity. A notable example is the United States' military Hall/North system, which in 1833 marked both the first United States percussion arm, and the Army's first breechloader. In 1841, the breech-loading Dreyse needle gun, which combined the projectile and powder together in a combustible cartridge, was adopted in Germany as the first military bolt-action gun.

The Civil War saw the adoption of a wide variety of percussion-based breech-loading systems, including those made by Sharps, Maynard, Burnside, and many others. Each system employed a proprietary cartridge, in the Sharps it was made of nitrated paper or linen, and with the others, a metallic cartridge was pierced for ignition. The first American bolt-action rifle, developed by Lieutenant Colonel Durrell Greene, was to receive only limited civilian or military acceptance in its ca. 1863 underhammer percussion format.

The Self-Contained Cartridge

Percussion arms could represent an effective repeating firearm, but what was needed was a self-contained cartridge with the primer, powder, and bullet all in one neat and weatherproof unit. An early attempt at this was the pinfire system, first introduced around 1846, in which a firing pin was mounted on each copper-cased cartridge, igniting an internal primer when struck by the gun's hammer. Although it gained a good deal of popularity in Europe, it never caught on much in the United States, with the external pin on each round being a bit cumbersome and hazardous.

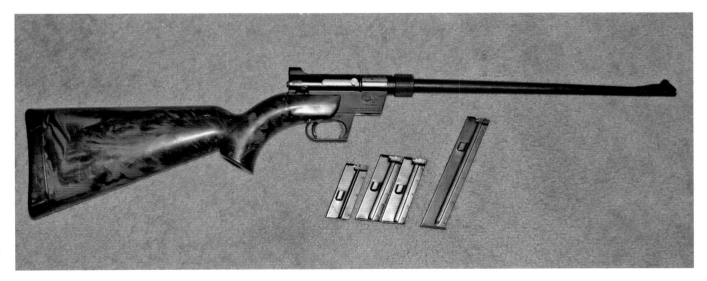

Example of an ArmaLite AR-7 survival rifle with 8-, 10-, and 15-round magazines.

Introduction

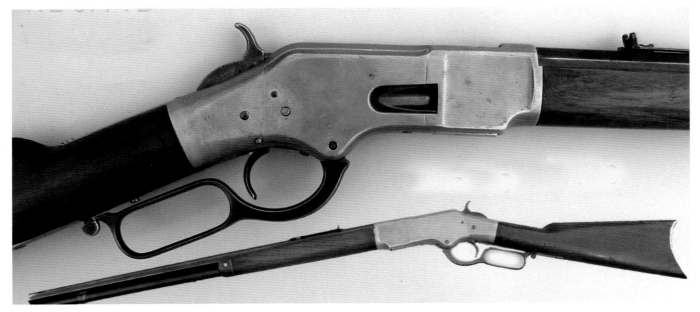

The Winchester Model 1866 was an early repeating rifle success. The distinctive brass frame earned it the nickname "Yellowboy" among the tribes of the American West, where it was a rapid-firing success.

The military has often been slow to embrace firearms innovation, preferring tried and true technology over the new and untested, and this was certainly true during the Civil War and Indian Wars era. Winchester had abandoned the rocket ball system in favor of a .44 rimfire cartridge in its famous brass-framed Henry rifle in 1860, but only a few were purchased and used during the Civil War. The Spencer Repeating Rifle Company had also patented an effective lever-action repeater that fired metallic cartridges by the beginning of the Civil War, but its adoption by the Army was resisted until it was demonstrated to President Lincoln, who promptly and personally championed its purchase. Although the Spencer was the most widely used repeating long gun of the Civil War, and breech-loading single-shot Sharps rifles in the hands of expert "Sharpshooters" took a toll, the vast majority of the soldiers on both sides were armed with muzzle-loading percussion muskets.

Rifles of the American West

With the post-war westward expansion, civilian demand was for the new repeating metallic-cartridge firearms. Winchester responded, with an improved brass frame rimfire Model 1866 lever action, followed by a centerfire Model 1873, and then by Models 1876 and 1886, made strong to handle true big-game cartridges in the .45-70 class. Marlin was Winchester's strongest competitor in the field, with Whitney-Kennedy and Evans also producing lever-action repeaters. Pump-action repeaters, including Colt's Lightning models, were offered in several frame sizes and calibers.

Despite the development of repeaters, single-shot rifles remained a popular option, and in the early years of metallic cartridges, they could handle stronger rounds than the repeaters. The tradition of powerful, big-bore rifles for the large game of the American west such as bison, elk, and grizzly bear certainly predates the Civil War. As first trappers and mountain men, and then settlers and farmers pushed into the Great Plains and Rocky Mountains, a new type of American rifle was developed to meet the need.

The percussion Plains Rifle was shorter than its predecessor — the longer and more slender Kentucky rifle — and was easier to handle on horseback and in brush. It took a heavier, larger-diameter ball appropriate to the larger game, which necessitated a heavier barrel, the weight of which was another factor dictating a shorter length. The Plains Rifle tended to have a half-stock, with the wood only cradling the rear half of the barrel. As befits a working gun, decoration tended to be minimal or nonexistent.

In the years preceding the Civil War, Plains Rifles by prominent makers such as Hawken and Gemmer, both of St. Louis, were eagerly sought after by long hunters and pilgrims heading west.

After the war, converted Sharps using centerfire metallic cartridges (including the .50-90 or "Sharps big 50") were perhaps the quintessential "buffalo rifles." Other popular single shots included the Winchester Model 1885 High Wall and Low Wall rifles; Stevens Ideal rifles, and the sturdy Remington Rolling Block rifles. Most were offered in a variety of frame sizes, barrel lengths, and weights, and calibers ranging from .22 rimfire to the .40 to .50 caliber rounds favored by commercial hunters. Various sights were available, from simple through elaborate, and stocking options included fairly straightforward ones through ornate buttplates and triggerguard configuration favored for Scheutzen-style target competitions. The single shot was generally considered to be more accurate than early repeaters, and so was favored for target competition and other precision work.

The American West of 1865 to 1900 is perhaps one of the most popular and romanticized eras of American history, with the lore of cowboys and Indians, lawmen and outlaws figuring large in our collective imagination. The military's resistance to new concepts continued into the Indian War years of the late nineteenth century. Even when repeating rifles with sixteen or more rounds that could be fired as fast as you could work the lever were available, the Army retained a single shot as its primary issue long arm. One concern cited was that soldiers armed with repeaters might expend ammunition too rapidly in the heat of battle.

Vast quantities of now-obsolete muzzleloaders remained in inventory from the Civil War. A method was developed to convert these to breech-loading cartridge rifles by cutting open the rear of the barrel and installing a breechblock that could be flipped open to load cartridges and remove empty brass like a trapdoor. When manufacture of new rifles resumed, they were based on the same system, and the "Trapdoor Springfield" single shot became the standard military

An example of a BAR (Browning Automatic Rifle) 30-60.

rifle from 1873 through the beginning of the Spanish American War in the late 1890s. In defense of the Army's decision, the trapdoor's .45-70 cartridge was significantly more powerful, with longer effective range than anything available in a repeater in the early 1870s.

After Custer's defeat at Little Big Horn, there was a vigorous debate over the military's choice of weapons. Some of the Indian victors had been using repeating rifles. One school of thought contended that if Custer's men had been armed with lever-action rifles instead of trapdoors, the outcome might have been different, although that conclusion is hard to support in light of the vastly outnumbered Seventh Cavalry's forces and strategic choices.

Birth of the Modern Rifle

While the U.S. market was well satisfied with lever-action repeating rifles, a different repeating mechanism gained favor with the armies of Europe. When the switch to metallic cartridges began, many European single-shot rifles used a "bolt-action" breech-loading system. In bolt-action rifles, a bolt handle extending from the breechblock is lifted up to unlock the breech and pulled to the rear, sliding it and allowing a cartridge to be loaded into the chamber in the rear of the barrel. The bolt handle is pushed forward and then down, engaging locking lugs to close the action while the rifle is fired. Single-shot bolt-action rifles adopted by militaries included the Chassepot (France 1866), Vetterli (Switzerland 1869), Berdan (Russia 1870), Beaumont (Netherlands 1871), and the Mauser (Germany 1871). Of these, the seeds of greatness lay in the last, the invention of brothers Peter and Paul Mauser.

The earliest military bolt-action repeating rifles used tubular magazines under the barrel, similar to the system on most American lever actions. The Portuguese Kropatschek in 1878 was among the first of this type. Mauser's tubular magazine repeater was first produced in 1884 as the German Model 1871/84. In 1885, smokeless powder was invented, and would lead to dramatic changes in firearms and ammunition design.

Military Innovations—Smokeless Powder and Jacketed Bullets

Smokeless powder, as the name implies, had the military advantage of not generating a cloud of smoke when fired. Black-powder smoke would reveal a shooter's position and, after a few rounds, develop a haze that could begin to obscure his vision. Another advantage was that smokeless powder produced far less fouling after shots than blackpowder, meaning that more shots could be fired before cleaning, and that powder debris was less likely to clog an action.

Its most important quality was that when ignited, its gases would expand more rapidly, creating higher pressures and driving the bullet to a higher velocity when it left the muzzle. As a bullet approaches 2,000 feet per second (about the speed of sound), its wounding capacity increases dramatically, allowing a lighter, smaller diameter projectile to have the same "stopping power" as a larger heavier round at a slower speed. The faster, smaller diameter, bullet will also have further range and a flatter trajectory. A bullet leaving the muzzle of the gun does not fly straight. From the instant it departs the barrel it is "falling" toward the ground due to the effect of gravity. A gun's sights are adjusted so the barrel is actually pointed very slightly up, giving a slight rainbow like curve to the bullet's path. A faster lighter bullet will travel further before gravity pulls it to earth, and a smaller diameter bullet has less wind resistance. The flatter

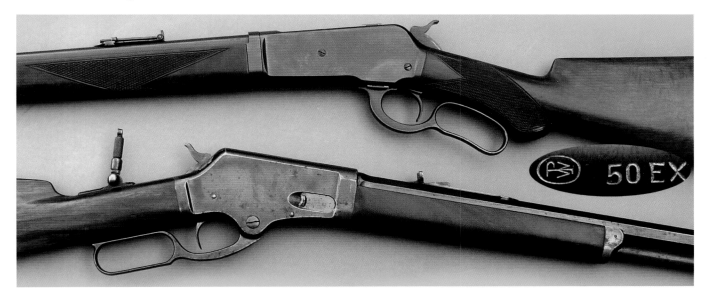

The lever-action repeating rifle became a favorite in the American West in the late 1800s, as continually improving designs allowed chambering of more powerful cartridges. Examples include this Winchester Model 1886 in the big .50 Express chambering, and Marlin Model 1881 in .45-70 caliber.

Throughout American history the firearm has been a working tool for farmers, ranchers, homesteaders, and outdoorsmen to provide food and eliminate pests and varmints. This Winchester Model 1890 pump-action .22 rifle was used on a farm by a Native American family to good effect, and shows a skillfully made custom wood stock and wooden scope cover constructed by its owners.

trajectory means it will be on target over a longer distance.

In general terms, the caliber of a bullet refers to a rough measurement of its diameter, expressed either in decimal fractions of an inch or millimeters. For example, a .45 caliber cartridge takes a bullet approximately 45/100" in diameter, which would also be very roughly 11 mm in diameter.Firearms designers took advantage of the new smokeless powder, using a smaller bullet closer to 1/3" diameter (ranging from under 7 mm to 9 mm with 8 mm most popular). Heavy lead would still be used to form the core of the bullet, but it would be encased in a harder copper or brass metal jacket so it would not quickly foul the rifling in the bore with soft lead that rubbed off at the higher velocities.

The first such bolt-action repeating rifle and smokeless smaller-caliber ammunition combination

Examples of rare 20th Century military rifles include the Pedersen semiautomatic (top), an early competitor of the Garand; and a Chinese Mukden bolt action Mauser pattern rifle.

to be adopted by a military was the 8 mm French Lebel bolt action in 1886. The pointed "Spitzer" bullet design is much more aerodynamically efficient than a round-nose design, offering better accuracy at longer ranges. However, when such cartridges are loaded nose-to-tail in a tube magazine, there is a danger that the pointed nose of one bullet will ignite the primer of the cartridge in front of it when the rifle recoils. Use of a box type magazine, where the cartridges are stacked parallel with one on top of the other overcomes this obstacle to the use of Spitzer bullets. The British Lee Metford bolt action, generally based on the Mauser concept, in .303 caliber used such a boxmagazine in 1888, and in 1889 Mauser produced its own 8 mm box-magazine rifle.

Another early boxmagazine repeater was the Mauser and Mannlicher-influenced German 1888 Commission rifle in 8 mm, which rapidly became a staple design; while the Austrians adopted a straight-pull bolt-action Steyr Mannlicher repeater in 8 mm the same year. Mid-bore bolt-action box-magazine designs rapidly followed, such as the Danish Krag Jorgensen in 1889 (with the United States adopting a Krag-based design in 1892), and the Swiss straight-pull Schmidt Rubin in the same year. The year 1891 saw the adoption of the Lebel pattern Mosin Nagant by Russia, the 6.5 mm Italian Carcano, and the 8 mm French Berthier.

During this period, military bolt actions were often modified to incorporate the new advances, and numerous military rifles from the turn of the century or slightly later are bolt-action single shots converted to magazine-fed repeaters, or were large-bore barrels relined to smaller calibers. The pinnacle of the bolt-action design is believed by many to be the Mauser

A modern Ruger PC4 with a selection of ammunition.

98, introduced in 1898. Improvements include cocking on opening of the bolt rather than closing, an added safety lug, and a larger chamber ring. This basic design became the basis of many, if not all, subsequent bolt-action military and sporting rifles, and variations served as primary rifles for many countries through World War II.

The tried and true United States Model 1903 that served with distinction through two world wars, with its "thirty ought six" (.30-'06) chambering, is basically a modified Mauser 1898 design. Modern production sporting rifles such as the classic Winchester Model 70, and bolt actions by Remington, Ruger, and others can trace their lineage to the Gewehr 98.

John Moses Browning

At this point in the history of firearms, we must travel back across the Atlantic, and back a few years in time to track the career of probably the greatest firearms inventor of all time, John Moses Browning of Ogden, Utah.

We've already mentioned one of Browning's earliest designs, the Winchester 1885 Single-Shot rifle. Others brought the Winchester lever-action repeaters into the smokeless powder era, first with the slim and handy Model 1892; followed by the Model 1894 which, with its "thutty-thutty" (.30-30) cartridge, became America's classic deer rifle; and the Model 1895 whose box magazine allowed the chambering of true high-power smokeless rifle cartridges with Spitzer bullets in a lever-action repeater. With a pump- or slide-action firearm, the shooter pulls back on the wooden forearm and then pushes it forward to eject the empty shell and replace it with a loaded one.

Browning had earlier applied the principle to a handy little .22 rifle for Winchester, the classic Model 1890, which remained popular for decades, happily employed in shooting galleries, used by squirrel and

A pair of well-worn AK47s.

Introduction

United States Military rifles have included (top to bottom) the Krag with its distinctive side-mounted box magazine (1892-1903); the 1903 Springfield bolt action (1903-WWII); the M1 Garand semiautomatic .30-06 battle rifle (1936-1957); and the light, handy M1 Carbine (1941-1957).

rabbit hunters, and good for all around "plinking." It was in the area of automatic firearms, however, that Browning probably made his greatest advances. Auto-loaders use part of the force of the firing cartridge to eject the empty casing and load a fresh round into the chamber. This may occur by direct or delayed blowback of the breechblock, by utilizing the recoil of the gun, or by redirecting some of the expanding gases of the burning gunpowder from the barrel to operate the action.

World War II Marks a Change

Most countries entered WWII with a bolt-action as their primary battle rifle.

Germany had its latest Mauser, the 8 mm Kar 98; Britain had the Short Magazine Lee Enfield (SMLE) in .303 caliber; Japan had the Arisaka; and so forth. The Springfield '03 was still widely issued to American forces, but in the decade preceding the outbreak of hostilities, the U.S. army had been first to test competing designs of semiautomatic rifles, and then

proceed with the manufacture and issue of the pattern deemed best.

The United States M1 Garand in .30-'06 caliber was without question the finest full power rifle fielded in WWII. Instead of a fixed or detachable box magazine, it was loaded with eight rounds held in a metal clip. When the last round was fired, the clip was automatically ejected with the action remaining open for quick insertion of another loaded clip. It was rugged, reliable, and powerful. It was also heavy. The army sought a weapon that was more accurate and powerful, and had a longer range than a pistol, but which was lighter and handier than the full-size rifle, intended primarily as a secondary weapon for tankers, artillery crews, and personnel who were not in a primary combat role. This role was filled by the M1 Carbine, a semiautomatic accepting a fifteen-round detachable box magazine. It fired a new straight-wall cartridge, midway in power between the pistol and the full-sized rifle.

A close-up shot of the bolt action on a Holland .374.

Germany also was developing a mid-range shoulder weapon, but with a different intent. They sought a detachable magazine rifle that would fire a reduced power cartridge and would be controllable and effective in full-auto firing mode, with more range and power than a submachine gun. The resulting MP-43 filled the bill, but was developed late in the war. The concept was one that would survive the conflict –the Germans called the weapon a "Sturmgewehr, " loosely translated as "assault rifle."

Most military establishments hesitated to "downsize" the power and range of their primary rifles in the early Cold War years. The semiautomatic detachable magazine concept was an obvious success, and there was something to be said for full-auto capability. A series of full power "battle rifles" were introduced to meet this need–the FN-FAL and the Heckler and Koch G3 being two patterns that were widely adopted. The United States developed a Garand look-alike with detachable magazine and full auto capability, the M14. However, the assault rifle concept wouldn't go away. The Soviet Union accepted the lower power round idea in its fixed magazine semiautomatic chambered for an intermediate power 7.62 x 39 mm round in 1945, the SKS, which saw wide distribution and production in Soviet client states, and enjoys popularity in the post-cold war United States as an inexpensive semiautomatic military surplus rifle.

They followed two years later with what would become probably the most widely produced military long-arm design in history, and the quintessential assault rifle–the Kalashnikov-designed AK-47, in the same caliber. The AK-47 is a select fire (semiautomatic or full-automatic) carbine size weapon with a detachable 20 or 30 round box magazine. It has a well-

deserved reputation for inexpensive manufacture, and for reliability even in the most adverse environments, or when used by under-trained indigenous forces who may neglect maintenance. It makes extensive use of sheet metal stampings in its construction, with a simple wooden buttstock with pistol grip.

The United States' version of the assault-weapon configuration was introduced in 1963, originally known as the AR-15 and XM-16 designed by Eugene Stoner. It was ultimately adopted as the M16 manufactured by Colt. It is chambered for the 5.56 mm NATO round, a military twin of the .223 Remington cartridge, and takes a detachable box magazine of 20 or 30 rounds. The rear sight is mounted on a distinctive integral carrying handle, and the stock and handguard are made of black synthetic material. Initial reviews of the M16 were mixed. A combination of an improper type of powder used in cartridge manufacture and a mistaken belief that maintenance could be neglected resulted in some early failures in the field. Some in the military establishment resisted a .22 caliber round for combat, dismissing it as not appropriate for two-legged targets.

This concern may be understood by reviewing a statistic commonly used to summarize a cartridge's power level–the muzzle energy. Muzzle energy is a product of the weight of the bullet and its velocity at the moment it leaves the barrel, expressed in foot pounds. The World War II and early post-war battle rifles chambered for .30-'06 and 8 mm Mauser class cartridges typically develop 2,000 to 2,600 ft./lbs. of muzzle energy. By contrast, the .45 ACP and 9 mm Luger rounds commonly used in military pistols and submachine guns run in the 300 to 400 ft./lb. range. That's nothing to sneeze at by the way… the common

Introduction

An H & K MR556 with an example of various accessories.

.22 Long Rifle cartridge which can certainly be lethal runs in the 90 to 125 ft./lb. range.

The intermediate "assault rifle" cartridges such as the 7.62 x 39 mm and 5.56 mm NATO average in the 1,200 to 1,600 ft./lb. range. As you can see, the designers of these were effective in "splitting the difference" between the high-power rifle and pistol cartridge power ranges, but many old soldiers were not sold on the compromise.

On the other hand, both M16 rifle and ammunition were significantly lighter than either the old battle rifles, or the AK system, allowing an infantryman to carry more ammunition or other load, and with tuning and evolution, the M16 pattern proved to be highly accurate out to distances reached by the earlier full-sized battle rifles.

The evolutionary descendants of the AK-47 and M16 have become the dominant military rifle patterns as the world enters the twenty-first century. Both have proven to be effective in combat. Semiautomatic versions of both designs have become highly popular with civilian shooters in recent decades, with the AR-15 (semiautomatic version of the M16) coming to dominate many types of target competition. In modern times, submachine guns and carbines have evolved to bridge the gap between handgun and full-sized rifle applications for law enforcement and military roles.

In the seventies, antigun forces incorrectly applied the "assault rifle" terminology to these semiautomatic sporting versions. The function of the sporters is identical to other semiautomatic sporting guns—it takes a separate pull of the trigger to fire each round. They lack the full-automatic (selective-fire) capability that originally defined "assault rifles."

However, the redefinition stuck, leading to ill-conceived legislation that temporarily banned the production of certain types of guns based solely on cosmetic appearances. Fortunately, the 1994 semiautomatic ban has since lapsed, making these popular semiautomatic rifles again available in their original configuration at affordable prices. Several states still regulate these arms on basis of magazine capacity.

Modern Rifle Milestones

Recent decades have witnessed the continuing evolution and development of other types of sporting firearms, with several recurring trends.

Probably the last of the great firearms inventor/entrepreneurs in the tradition of Sam Colt and D. B. Wesson was Bill Ruger. Partnering with Alexander Sturm to create Sturm Ruger Inc., their company continues to create rugged, inexpensive, yet classic sporting gun designs, including the 10-22 and Mini-14 rifles. Among the company's newest innovations–a piston-based semiautomatic rifle configured on the AR-15.

Other new firms sprang up to challenge the old line makers with improved or cheaper versions of the classic designs. Springfield Armory has become a major maker of military pattern sporting arms based on classic military designs such as the M14 and M1 Garand patterns. Firms such as Bushmaster, DPMS, LMT, and others began to develop a reputation for quality AR-15 semiautomatic rifles, a market once belonging to Colt. Other makers such as Uberti and Navy Arms saw the strong nostalgia market for nineteenth century designs, and began to produce quality versions of Winchester lever guns, and other arms appealing to Old West buffs and participants in the fun new sport of Cowboy Action Shooting.

Options for aiming a rifle have expanded dramatically over the past 50 years. Telescopic sights for precision rifle shooting were used as early as the Civil War. However, it wasn't until after World War II that it became a standard practice to mount a scope on most serious hunting rifles, and the technology of these optics has continually evolved and improved. New forms of sighting equipment such as electronic red-dot sights, tritium (glow-in-the-dark) night sights, laser-aiming systems, and even night-vision scopes are widely available.

Enjoying Firearms

Firearms ownership and usage is a treasured American tradition. There are two fundamental requirements for those who would participate in this experience.

The first requirement is of course safety. Everyone needs to know the basic safety rules by heart. There are many, but the following, if committed to memory and followed religiously, will prevent tragic mishaps:

1. Treat every firearm as if it is loaded.
2. Never let the muzzle point at anything you are not willing to see destroyed.
3. Do not touch the trigger until your sights are on target.
4. Be sure of your target, and what is beyond it. Firearms projectiles can travel long distances, and will penetrate many visual barriers.
5. Keep your firearms so they are not accessible to unauthorized, untrained, or irresponsible individuals.

Even folks who choose not to own guns need to be sure their children understand basic gun safety. For the smallest kids, the National Rifle Association (NRA)'s Eddy Eagle program has a basic, easy-to-remember drill for what they should do if they come across a gun:

1. Stop!
2. Don't touch.
3. Leave the area.
4. Tell an adult.

If you choose to own a firearm, get instruction in how to use it safely and effectively. Even if you don't own a gun, such training can still be a good idea, as it may some day be as vital to you or a loved one as training in CPR.

The NRA is the largest firearms training organization in the world, and offers solid programs for folks from beginning to advanced shooters. Ask a local gun shop, gun club, shooting range, or police department to put you in touch with an NRA-certified program.

This brings us to the second requirement for firearms owner: Vigilance.

There is a special genius to the U.S. Constitution's Bill of Rights, which protects the individual and collective civil rights of Americans. It is no mistake that the second amendment to that document provides that "the right of the people to keep and bear arms shall not be infringed."

If it were not for the NRA, that basic human right would have been lost long ago. It's an ongoing battle; not always an easy or popular one, but an essential one nonetheless.

Close up of a Kimber Model 8400 Super America rifle and a selection of cartridges.

Anschütz

The Anschütz Company is known as a leading manufacturer of precise accurate target rifles. For the past forty years, more than eighty-five percent of all Olympic small-bore rifle medalists and more than 95 percent of the World Class Biathlon medalists have used Anschütz rifles.

The Anschütz Company had its humble beginnings more than 150 years ago, in 1856, in Zella-Mehlis, Thuringia, Germany. The founder of the company, Johann Heinrich Gottlieb Anschütz, planned to manufacture Flobert and pocket pistols and shotguns. By 1896, the small firm had seventy-six employees and opened its own factory. Although the founder, J. G. Anschütz died in 1901, his two sons, Fritz and Otto, carried on in the family trade.

The brothers continued to expand the company; by 1911 they had 200 employees. Although by 1935, both of the brothers were dead, Fritz's two sons presided over a company with 500 employees. In 1945 after World War II, the company was dismantled.

In 1950, J. G. Anschütz GmbH was refounded in Ulm as a small firm with seven employees and only twenty pieces of equipment. At first they concentrated on producing air pistols and doing repairs on firearms. Soon the company had grown to 250 employees producing target rifles. In 1968, the fourth generation of the family, in the person of Dieter Anschütz, was at the helm of the firm. Today, Jochen Anschütz is the head of the company, the fifth generation of his family. The company now also produces a line of shooting jackets, boots, gloves, optics, and many shooting accessories.

1780 Classic

8001 Cub

1907

1827 Fortner

1770D

1770D with Scope

LaserPower

ArmaLite

ArmaLite was founded in Hollywood, California, in 1954 as a division of Fairchild Engine and Airlane Corporation. The company was set up mainly by Fairchild employee, George Sullivan.

For more than half a century, there had been little development in small arms—most of the interest and changes were with the semiautomatic rifles and machine guns. The AR-5 .22 Hornet Survival Rifle was ArmaLite's first major new product. The U.S. Air Force soon adopted the AR-5 as the MA-1 Survival Rifle.

Through the remainder of the 1950s, ArmaLite focused on the development and manufacture of military firearms and the creation of modern lightweight weapons employing newly developed plastics and alloys.

In 1961 Fairchild was having financial difficulties and the principals of the ArmaLite division were able to purchase the company. ArmaLite switched its emphasis and embarked on a new phase in the company's growth, as ArmaLite Incorporated.

In 1983 ArmaLite was sold to Elisco Tool Manufacturing Company in the Philippines. In 1995 ArmaLite was reorganized yet again and production facilities were set up in Illinois.

AR10 Super SASS2

AR50 A1

AR30 M

ARM15 A2

ARM15 A4 Carbine

AR10 A4 CBF

AR10 BNF .338

M15 7.62 x 39

M15 6.8 Carbine

Baikal

Baikal—Federal State Unitary Plant "IZHEVSKY MEKHANICHESKY ZAVOD" (FSUP "IMZ")—is one of the largest businesses within the Russian Agency on Conventional Armament.

In 1944 the first production facility went into operation, producing motorcycles, mining equipment, and scales.

From 1945 to 1955, the company produced more than five million of the new army Makarov pistols, one of the best of its kind. Also during this period, in 1949, the company began the manufacture of the ZK simple single-barrel model and the IZH-49 double-barrel gun. The Baikal plant became one of the largest manufacturers of sporting and hunting guns in the world.

An important hallmark not only for the company but also for firearms manufacturing in general was the 1956 opening of the Gunsmithing and Engraving School to train qualified gunmakers.

The intervening decades were devoted to the production of a wide range of firearms and other products for the Soviet military. The number of government orders greatly decreased by 1990, and Baikal turned its attention to increasing its manufacture and types of hunting, sporting and personal firearms.

In the 1990s, Baikal for the first time was able to export products to the United States. The legendary Makarov pistol was replaced by the 9 mm Yarygin army pistol in 2000. Today Baikal firearms are available in more than sixty-five countries.

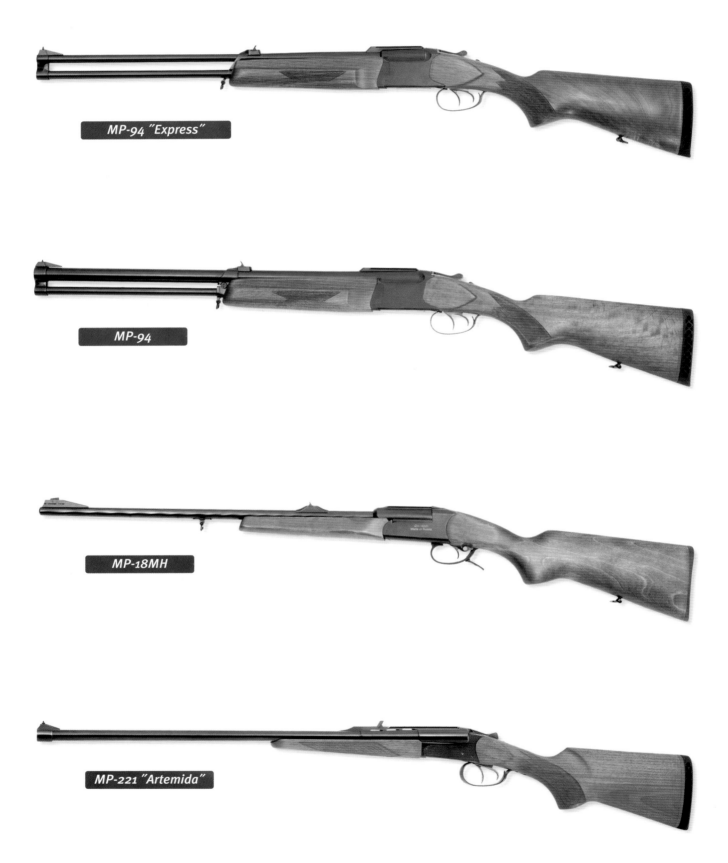

MP-94 "Express"

MP-94

MP-18MH

MP-221 "Artemida"

MP-94 "Sever"

MP-94MP

MP-161K

Benelli

Founded in 1967, the Italian arms manufacturer, Benelli Armi SpA, is located in Urbino, Italy. The six Benelli brothers were famous for Fratelli Benelli, a company founded in 1911 to produce motorcycles. By 1967, the Benelli brothers' passion for hunting had led them from motorcycles to the production of a quality automatic shotgun capable of firing five rounds per second, making it the fastest gun in the world. The concept and development of this revolutionary firearm was the work of designer, Bruno Civolani who created a unique inertia system which remains the basis for many of the Benelli guns produced today.

The firm is renowned the world over for superior shotguns favored by military, law enforcement, and civilians. Many United States SWAT teams prefer the Benelli M3 12 gauge. In recent years, Benelli developed the Benelli M4 Super 90, a remarkable gas-operated semiautomatic shotgun designed for military use in urban settings. In 2000, Pietro Benelli became the owner of Benelli and Benelli USA.

A favorite choice for waterfowl hunters is the Benelli Super Black Eagle, one of the first semiautomatic shotguns capable of firing the 2.75-, 3-, and 3.5-inch shotgun shells. In 1993, Tom Knapp, recognized as one of the foremost exhibition shooters of today, joined Team Benelli, a group of professional shooters who use only Benelli firearms. Knapp holds three world shooting records for hand-held clay targets. His most recent record was set in October 2004 when he shot an incredible ten clay pigeons in 2.2 seconds using the Benelli ComforTech M2 Field gun.

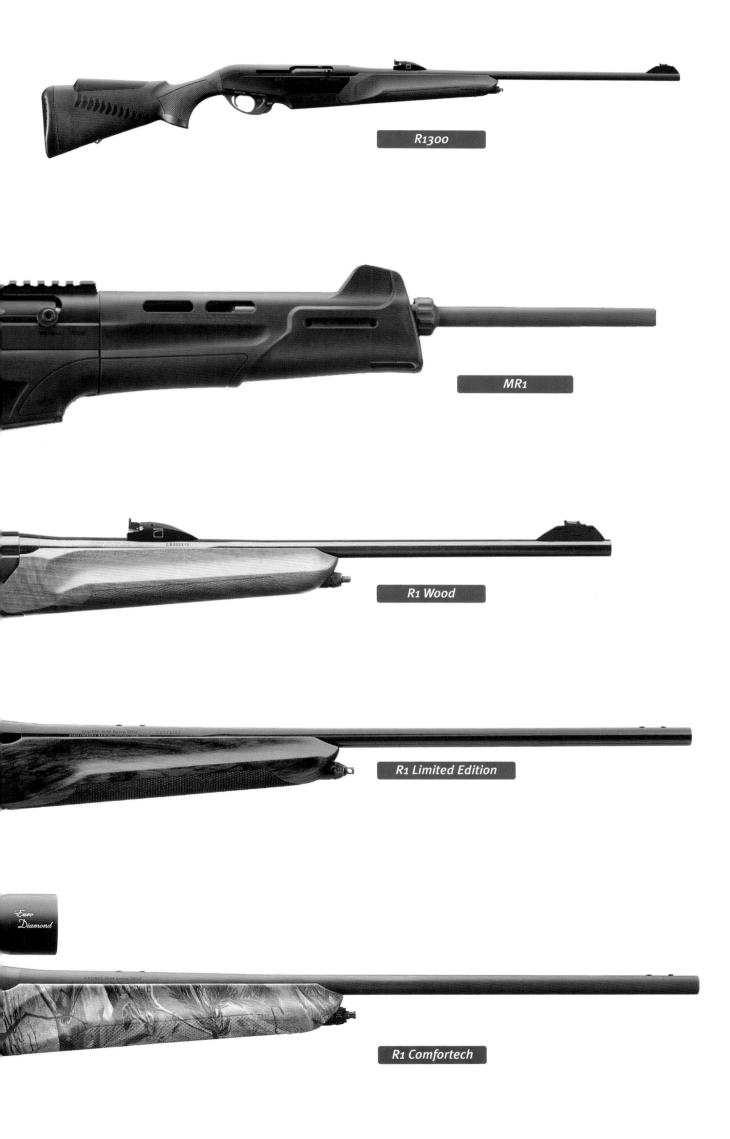

R1300

MR1

R1 Wood

R1 Limited Edition

R1 Comfortech

Beretta

Founded in 1526, Beretta is one of the oldest corporations in the world. For almost 500 years, Beretta has been owned by the same family. The earliest bill of sale in the company archives indicates that in 1526, gunsmith Maestro Bartolomeo Beretta of Gardone Val Trompia (Brescia, Lombardy, Italy) sold 185 arquebus (heavy musket needing to be propped up by supports) barrels to the Arsenal of Venice. Over the span of nearly five centuries, Beretta developed from a small guild operation making exquisitely detailed and precision-handmade firearms to an international firm trading in more than 100 countries and using the most modern forms of manufacture, including robotics.

By the twentieth century, the company was producing both military and sporting firearms. This marked the onset of decades of incredible growth. At the end of the nineteenth century, Beretta had 130 employees and a single 10,000-square-foot factory. By 2000, its factories took up more than 75,000 square feet of space in Gardone and another 50,000 square feet at sites in Italy, Spain, and the United States (Maryland).

During World War II, Beretta manufactured rifles and pistols for the Italian military until the 1943 Armistice between Italy and the Allied forces. The Germans still controlled the northern part of Italy, and they seized the Beretta factories and continued producing arms until 1945.

In the 1950s, Beretta expanded into automobile and motorcycle production. A true indication of its international fame came in the 1960s, however, when Ian Fleming's master spy, James Bond 007, carried a 25-caliber Beretta in both books and film.

Today, the company is owned and is run by Ugo Gussalli Beretta (a direct descendant of Bartolomeo) and his sons, Franco and Pietro. One of the world's great arms producers, Beretta makes more than 1,500 pieces each day, ranging from portable firearms (shotguns for hunting and competition, pump-action guns, semiautomatic pistols, and assault rifles). Although more than ninety percent of their production is in sporting firearms, Beretta also supplies arms to the Italian military, the U.S. Armed Forces and State Police, France's Gendarmerie Nationale and the French Air Force, the Spanish Guardia Civil, and the Turkish Police Force, among others.

The parent company, Beretta Holding, controls Beretta USA, Benelli, Franchi, SAKO, Stoeger, Tikka, Uberti, the Burris Optics Company, and a twenty percent interest of the Browning arms company.

Sako 85 Bavarian

Sako 85 Classic

Sako 85 Varmint Laminated

Sako 85 Varmint

Sako 85 Hunter

Sako 85 Finnlight

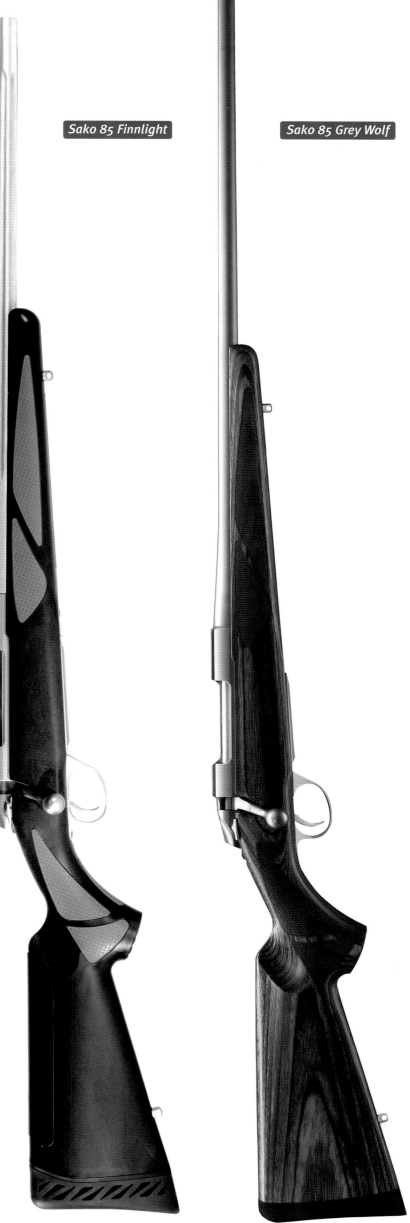

Sako 85 Grey Wolf

Sako TRG

Tikka T3 Varmint

Sako Quad

T3 Hunter

T3 Lite Stainless

Tikka T3 Lite

Blaser

More than 50 years ago, gunsmith Horst Blaser oversaw the development of a light and safe over and under rifle–shotgun combination, the Blaser "Diplomat." He did not have the skills or facility to actually manufacture his creation and so many components were manufactured in Ferlach, Austria, giving the Diplomat distinctive "Ferlach," touch such as barrels being completely soldered together up to the monoblock. Safety was assured by the single lock, with a manual cocking lever.

A slightly more advanced model, the Blaser 60, had a single lock-up wedge. It became the first German hunting rifle to be machine-manufactured. Improving and enhancing the Blaser 60 even further, Blaser developed the ES 63. ES stands for "Einschloss" meaning "single lock." The receiver and monoblock

were enlarged to allow for a wider range of calibers.

The ES63 was supplied with a 12-gauge shotgun barrel and also a range of rifle calibers from .22 lfb to 5.6 x 52 R. A new uncocked lock, gave the rifle the maximum safety typical of Blaser rifles. A classic claw mount was also used. The Diplomat was sold with great success through the rising hunting goods supplier Frankonia.

Horst Blaser redesigned the over and under rifle–shotgun combination "Diplomat," so that he could completely finish the production of the barrels himself –excluding making the barrel bore. Hence the model 60 with a single lockup-wedge was produced. This featured the barrels being soldered from the end of the fore-arm to the muzzle.

R8

R8 Professional

R93 Rimfire

K95 Baroness

R93 Safari

K95 Baroness Stutzen

Tactical 2

R93 Professional

Browning

The Browning Arms Company opened in Ogden, Utah, in 1927, one year after the death of John Moses Browning, the renowned gunsmith and firearms inventor from whom the company took its name. In 1852 Jonathon Browning, father of John, had set up his first gun store in Ogden. After Jonathon's death in 1872, John Moses Browning and his five brothers established Browning Brothers Company, a retail arms business. John Browning is known as the greatest firearms inventor in history.

Browning had 128 gun patents; during his years as an inventor more than 50 million guns were produced from those patents. His best known, and most widely sold guns, included the 45-caliber pistol, the 1895 Colt Peacemaker machine gun, the Browning automatic rifle, several 30- and 50-caliber machine guns, and the Browning Automatic-5 shotgun, which was first made in 1902 and is manufactured still today. The Browning Company also became well known for other products such as gun safes, knives, and shooting and hunting apparel.

The actual production of the guns eventually was handed over to a number of firearm manufacturers, including Winchester Arms, the Colt Arms Manufacturing Company, and the Fabrique Nationale of Belgium, the Remington Arms Company, and Savage Arms Company. All of these produce guns from John Browning's patents.

The Fabrique Nationale of Belgium purchased the company in 1977, but the world headquarters is still located just outside of Ogden, Utah, in Mountain Green. By 1989 the sales for the company exceeded $100 million just in the United States. Today Browning's company catalog includes sporting rifles and guns, knives, pistols, fishing gear, outdoor clothing, and golf clubs.

X-Bolt Medallion Open Sights

BAR Lightweight Stalker

A-Bolt Composite Stalker

A-Bolt Stainless M-1000 Eclipse

BAR Safari

BAR Zenith Prestige
Big Game

X-Bolt Hunter

X-Bolt Stainless
Stalker

A-Bolt Stalker
Composite

Browning

BAR Zenith Prestige Wood

BAR ShortTrac

BAR Zenith Ultimate

BAR LongTrac Realtree

*T-Bolt Composite
Sporter*

X-Bolt Medallion

*BAR Zenith
Custom*

Bushmaster

Bushmaster Firearms International has its home base in Windham, Maine. Semiautomatic pistol and rifle variants of the AR-15 design comprise Bushmaster's main line of firearms. Today, Bushmaster is the most popular brand of AR-type firearms in the United States.

From the start, Bushmaster Firearms developed and manufactured a "First Generation" rifle using a unique aluminum lower receiver while the upper receiver was constructed from stamped steel. The earliest examples utilized the AK-47 gas system with the recoil spring located within the upper barrel; this is in contrast to the AR-15/M-16, which has the recoil spring located within the buttstock. These First Generation rifles are rare collectibles today.

The Bushmaster Dissipator tried to combine an AR carbine with the long sight radius of the full-length M16A2 with the shorter (16.1"/406mm) barrel of some of the shorter carbines. This would permit the best use of the iron sights for a carbine with such a short barrel, and may be preferred if the carbine is going to be used primarily with iron sights.

Today Bushmaster Firearms International, produces a wide range of firearms for use in hunting, competition shooting, law enforcement, military, recreation, and home defense.

Carbon 15 M4 Custom

Carbon 15 9 mm Carbine

Gas Piston Rifle

BA50 Carbine

Carbon 15 M4 "Flat Top" Carbine

Optics Ready Carbine
with Iron Sights

.357 Magnum

MOE Dissipator

Modular Carbine with Ace
Skeleton Stock

Optics Ready Carbine

M4 A2 Type Carbine

Varminter

CheyTac

CheyTac® USA bases its product line on its motto "Seize the Distance" and is proud to call itself the leader in long-range precision rifle systems. CheyTac's main goal is the development and manufacture of tactical small arms and accompanying support systems. Unfortunately, many of the military small arms in use today were conceived more than fifty years ago when military tactics and combat were very different. The changing and evolving field tactics mandate the need for new concepts in weapon design and conception.

In addition to military firearms, CheyTac is also working very closely with Homeland Security in the United States to develop appropriate weapons lines and systems for their special needs.

The CheyTac® Intervention rifle along with the CheyTac® cartridge is at the core of their new long-range rifle systems. The rifle is a seven-shot repeating takedown rifle with removable barrel. The operator can tear down the entire rifle and replace barrels in the field. The system has undergone rigorous field testing and is capable of soft-target interdiction at a range of up to 2,500 yards.

To accomplish its mission, CheyTac® USA identifies talented individuals from various disciplines who are known to "think out of the box." They focus their energies on the design of quality, unique weaponry and support systems, which will allow the military and Homeland Security to execute new small-arm field tactics.

408 LER — A5 McMillan Stock

M300

M200 Intervention — Stock Retracted

375 LER — Aluminum Modular Stock

Christensen Arms

In 1985, after working for many years at Fibertek, an aerospace engineering company, Roland Christensen started his own company, Applied Composite Technology (ACT). ACT designs and markets a line of prosthetic feet and knee parts around the world. Most Paralympic athletes use ACT products. Taking full advantage of his Ph.D. degree in mechanical engineering from the University of Utah and his vast research and executive experience in several engineering firms, in 1995, he started a second, very different company, Christensen Arms, in Fayette, Utah, his hometown.

Christensen Arms specializes in custom firearms starting with their first product, the 22-250 caliber "Carbon One." This rifle featured a graphite-epoxy barrel casing. Along with the newly developed barrel, these light-weight guns use a unique titanium muzzle break, which serves to lessen the recoil by at least 50 percent. ACT's market for their high-end custom products are serious hunting and shooting enthusiasts. Christensen Arms has just launched a T.V. show on the "*Outdoor Channel*" entitled "Christensen Arms Outdoors".

CA-15

Hunter

Extreme

Carbon One Custom

Ranger R

Colt

Founded in Hartford, Connecticut, in 1847, Colt's Manufacturing Company (CMC, formerly Colt's Patent Firearms Manufacturing Company) is a U.S. firearms manufacturer famous for the development and production of a wide range of firearms including military and civilian arms.

The fame of the company was built on the patent held by Samuel Colt, who designed and produced the first working revolver, the Colt .45 or Single-Action Army or Peacemaker. This handgun would revolutionize the firearm world with its revolving cylinder that could hold five or six bullets. The gun was the most used firearm in the American West in the nineteenth century.

The preeminence of Colt in the firearms business of the latter half of the nineteenth century is evident in the post–Civil War slogan: "Abe Lincoln may have freed all men, but Sam Colt made them equal." The

Colt revolvers were often referred to as "the Great Equalizers" since they could be loaded and fired by almost anyone. It became the best-known firearm not only in North America but also in many European countries.

Although the M16 was not developed by Colt, they were for a long time responsible for its production along with other related firearms. Throughout the twentieth century, Colt continued to manufacture an innovative line of firearms.

In 2002 Colt Manufacturing Company split off a separate division—Colt Defense—to manufacture firearm lines exclusively for the military, law enforcement agencies, and private security firms around the world. Now Colt Manufacturing Company produces firearms and accessories solely for the civilian market of hunters and sports enthusiasts, and for home security.

SP 901

SP 6040

SP 6920

CR 6720

CR 6720

AR15 A2

AR15 A3

LE Carbine

M4

LE6920MP-FDE

SMG

Corner Shot

In 2002, two former Israeli Defense Force senior combat and special units' officers founded Corner Shot Holdings in Tel Aviv. They have developed a new technological system that adapts to the majority of handguns manufactured and in use today. The revolutionary concept allows for observing and engaging a subject from around a corner. This will allow security teams to protect themselves totally from being placed in the line of fire.

The system includes a small camera with an LCD monitor that can view and record the target from many angles and viewpoints. The camera can even be detached to scan an entire area. The Corner Shot system is also designed to include numerous accessories for specialized uses, including zoom, day–night and thermal cameras, audiovisual sets, lasers, and more.

Corner Shot 40

Corner Shot APR

Corner Shot 40

CZUB

The beginnings of Ceska zbrojovka Uherský Brod (CZUB) were in 1936, when it was established as a division of Ceska zbrojovka in the town of Uherský Brod in Czechoslovakia, now in the Czech Republic. The first firearms produced by the fledgling company were machine guns for aircraft, military pistols and small bore rifles. During the years of Nazi Occupation during World War II, the workers at the plant were made to produce and repairs weapons for the Germans. After the war, beginning in 1945, CZUB manufactured both military and civilian firearms

In 1950, the company became a totally separate government enterprise, "Presne strojirenstvi Uhersky Brod" (The Precision Machine Tooling Company), and was set up with a number of specialized subdivisions. During the decades of the Cold War, CZUB produced a range of military armaments including both rifles and pistols.

Through the 1970s and 1980s, the firm was merged with other companies and worked in producing airplane engines and tractors. .

By the 1990s, the company was once more an independent entity devoted to producing a range of firearms and reassuming the name eská zbrojovka, s.p. In 1992, the joint stock company Ceska zbrojovka a.s., Uhersky Brod was established in agreement with a Czech privatization project and the decentralization of government concerns. As it joined the economy of the free world, CZUB sold weapons in more than 60 countries. In 1997, it opened CZ-USA in the United States and continues to produce military, law enforcement and recreational firearms. Today, CZUB has more than 2000 employees and is one of the world's largest arms manufacturers.

455 Varmint Evolution

512

550 Carbine Kevlar

453 American

453 Varmint

452 Silhouette

452 Style

452 FS

452 Scout

452 American
with Scope

511

513 Basic

527 American S4

527 Carbine

527 M1 Ultralite Predator

550 Magnum H.E.T

750 Sniper

FNH

FNH, formally known as Fabrique Nationale Herstal, was founded in 1889 in the small town of Herstal outside of Liege in Belgium. Today "FN" is a subsidiary of the Herstal Group, which also owns U.S. Repeating Arms Company (Winchester) and Browning Arms Company.

In 1889 the company joined other arms manufacturers as a part of a company named Fabrique Nationale d'Armes de Guerre (FN) to help produce 150,000 Mauser Model 89 rifles ordered by the Belgian government.

In 1897 the company acquired the license for John Browning's 7.65 Browning pistol with its innovative locking system. This was the beginning of a long and productive collaboration between the Belgian company FN and Browning, the Utah inventor. In fact, Browning's son, Val, carries on his father's work with the company.

In the beginning of the twentieth century, FN also became involved in producing cars, motorcycles, and trucks. In 1914 the two bullets that killed the Archduke Ferdinand and set off World War I came from an FN Model 1910 semiautomatic pistol in 7.65 x 17 mm (.32 ACP).

In the 1930s, Browning designed his renowned .50 Cal M2 machine gun which is still manufactured by FN today.

In the later part of the twentieth century, FN helped to develop and produce both machine guns and light rifles used by NATO forces. Through to the present day, FN has continued to develop and produce innovative firearms and weapons systems that are deployed by the military by land, sea, and air.

PS90 TR (Triple Rail)
Semi-auto Carbine, Black

FS2000 Tactical
Semi-auto Carbine

MK 16 CQC

F2000 Tactical

FN A1a SPR

FN SPR A3 G

FN A5 M SPR

Holme 2087

MK16 Standard

FNAR Heavy Barrel

P90® TR Laser Visible (LV)

PS90 TR (Triple Rail) Semi-auto Carbine, OD Green

FN A1 SPR

FN TSR XP

FN A2 SPR

Harrington & Richardson

In 1871, Gilbert Harrington invented a top-breaking, shell-ejecting revolver to provide a firearm that was not only accurate and durable, but also had the added value of being easy to load and unload. In order to manufacture this new revolver, Harrington teamed with William Richardson to form Harrington & Richardson.

By 1893, the company's success allowed them to build a new plant in Worcester, Massachusetts. This enabled them to develop and produce a successful and revolutionary line of single-barrel shotguns with automatic shell-ejection features.

During World War I, H & R manufactured shoulder-held flare guns for the military. In 1932, a new pistol record was established using an H & R single-shot target pistol, which was later adopted for use by the United States Army. The company became a main provider of firearms for United States forces during World War II, manufacturing the M1 Garand rifle, the M14, and the M16.

In 1986, the company went out of business and a new firm was formed, Harrington and Richardson 1871. In 2000, Harrington and Richardson 1871 was purchased by Marlin Firearms Company. Today, Harrington and Richardson 1871 is part of the Remington Arms Company family, which manufactures several lines of firearms, particularly single-shot shotguns under two trademarks, New England Firearms and Harrington & Richardson.

Pardner

Ultra Hunter Thumbhole Stock Rifle

Sportster

Sportster™ Compact

Survivor® Blued

Handi-Rifle with Synthetic Stock

Handi-Rifle

Synthetic Handi-Rifle

Harrington & Richardson

Walnut HandiRifle

Ultra Hunter Rifle

60

Ultra Varmint Fluted

Ultra Varmint Thumb-hole Stock Rifle

Heckler & Koch

In 1949 three former Mauser Company engineers, Edmund Heckler, Theodor Koch, and Alex Seidel, joined together to form Heckler & Koch (H&K). In the early years, H&K made machine tools, parts for sewing machines, gauges, and other precision parts. By 1956 the firm was offering to produce the G3 automatic rifle for the Bundeswehr (German Federal Army).

Over the years since, H&K has designed and formulated more than one hundred weapons and creating a lightweight polymer line of assault rifles, the G36 of firearms for military and police organizations around the globe. In 1991 the company was bought by British Aerospace's Royal Ordinance division. Since then, their work in weaponry has mainly concentrated on modifying and perfecting the SA80 rifle series for the British Army and creating a line of lightweight polymer assault rifles, the G36.

In 2002, H&K was sold to a German group (H&K Beteiligungs-GmbH) that was created for the purpose of this acquisition.

Located in Oberndorf in Baden-Württemberg, H&K also has subsidiaries in the United Kingdom, France, and the United States. "Keine Kompromisse!" (No Compromise!) is the company's motto, emphasizing their desire to produce accurate reliable products with ergonomic efficiency, without sacrificing any one trait for the other. Today they provide firearms to the Special Air Service, U.S. Navy SEALs, Delta Force, FBI HRT, Kentucky State Police SRT, the German KSK and GSG 9, and many other counter-terrorist and hostage rescue teams. In 2004 the U.S. Department of Homeland Security awarded a contract to H&K for delivery of up to 65,000 pistols, the largest contract in United States law enforcement history.

HK 416 Compact

HK417

USC

SL8-6

MR 762

MR 556

HK 416 20

MSG 90 A1

PSG1A1 HKO

G36 ONG3

Henry Repeating Arms

Benjamin Tyler Henry was working for Winchester Arms when he patented his design for the first practical, lever-action repeating rifle. His innovative concept enabled one man to match the firepower of several men with muzzle-loading guns.

The manufacture of these guns in a factory in New Haven, Connecticut, coincided with the beginnings of the Civil War. Indeed, one of the earliest Henry rifles, serial number 6, was beautifully engraved and presented to President Abraham Lincoln. Today, that very rifle with the president's name engraved on the side plate is in the Smithsonian Institution in Washington, D.C. By the middle of 1862, Union soldiers were carrying the Henry rifle into battle against their Confederate countrymen. Most of the guns were privately purchased by the soldiers themselves; they retailed for between $32.00 and $80.00. This new design found favor not only with the soldiers but also with civilians.

The Henry rifle was made with a, 44-caliber rimfire cartridge which allowed not only very precise but also very rapid firing. The rifle could fire more than forty-five shots in less than one minute. The Henry rifle later played an important role in further expansion of settlers into the American West. During its term of production from 1860–1867, 14,094 rifles were manufactured and distributed.

"Modern Henry" rifles in various versions have been offered by several companies including Navy Arms. All are manufactured in limited production. The "Modern Henrys" are the firearm of choice for Civil War Reenactors and also has been use in films about the Old West such as *Dances with Wolves*.

Golden Boy Deluxe

Lever Action

Carbine .22 S-L-LR with Large Loop Lever

Lever Octagon .22 Magnum

.30-30 Brass Octagon

U.S. Survival Silver .22 LR

Pump Action .22 Magnum

US SURVIVAL

Henry Repeating Arms

Golden Boy .22 S-L-LR

Mini Bolt with Scope

Big Boy Deluxe Engraved
.44 Magnum

Big Boy .44 Magnum

Hi-Point

Hi-Point Firearms established its place in the firearms market by producing polymer-framed semiautomatic pistols, selling inexpensively and foregoing the aesthetics. Many of Hi-Point's pistols are heavy, but have few parts, making them easier to maintain. Instead of the more common breech-locking system, the pistols employ a heavy slide that keeps the breech closed through its size and weight. In the field, the pistols do require a special punch or screwdriver to permit field-stripping.

The slide itself is diecast from an alloy of aluminum, magnesium, and copper known as zamak-3. Most other slides are made from forged steel. Located in Mansfield, Ohio, Hi-Point favors the diecasting method since they are located in an area of Ohio that is home to many companies that manufacture diecast parts for automobiles, and Hi-Point has taken advantage of their presence.

Hi-Point carbines are also manufactured with a polymer stock, stamped sheet metal receiver cover, and a bolt cast from zamak-3. Steel, however, is used for the barrel of the carbine. They utilize blowback action usually most practical for a low-pressure carbine.

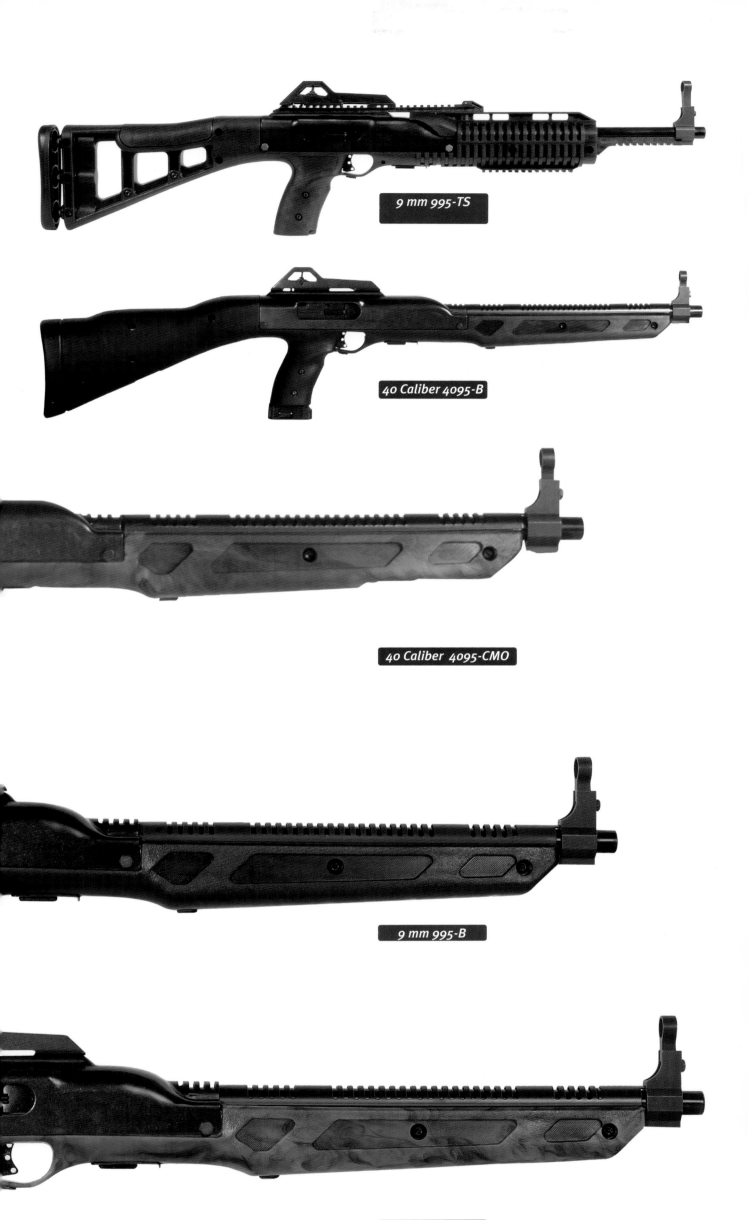

9 mm 995-TS

40 Caliber 4095-B

40 Caliber 4095-CMO

9 mm 995-B

9 mm 995-CMO

Kimber

In 1979 Greg and Jack Warne first established Kimber (originally known as "Kimber of Oregon") in Clackamas, Oregon, a suburb of Portland. The name came from Jack Warne's birthplace in Australia, Kimba-Abo (which means "bush fire"). Jack had been the head of Sporting Arms (SportCo) a premier firearms company he had started in Adelaide, Australia. In 1968 his company was bought out by Omark Industries, based in Portland, and Jack came to the United States as president of Omark.

Kimber's early reputation in the field was built on the quality of their .22-caliber long rifles patterned after the bolt-action Winchesters. Soon they needed to expand their manufacturing capabilities and so opened a second production facility in nearby Colton, Oregon. They also became renowned for their quality pistols, especially the 1911. Today, Kimber pistols are used by the LAPD SWAT teams, the U.S. Marines, and U.S. Rapid Shooting Olympic Team members.

Kimber has seen its share of financial difficulties and buyouts. In the mid-1990s, Greg Warne, one of the original founders of Kimber, started up Kimber of America with financial backing from Les Edelman. Edelman eventually bought out Warne's shares, and combined Kimber with one of his other companies that was suffering from a loss in defense contracts, Jerico Precision Manufacturing. He merged the two companies, moving Kimber to Yonkers, New York.

Today Kimber of America continues its rich tradition of producing and developing high-precision pistols and rifles for military, law enforcement, and personal use.

84M Pro Varmint

84M LongMaster Classic

84M LongMaster VT

84M LPT

Kimber

84M Montana

8400 Advanced Tactical

Sonora

8400 Talkeetna

8400 Caprivi

Model 84M Classic
Select Grade

Marlin

John M. Marlin worked for the Colt Company at their plant in Hartford, Connecticut, during the Civil War. By 1870, he had opened his own firearms manufacturing and marketing company in that same town. His first products were derringers and revolvers. He put together an amazing team of inventors who developed innovative models, some of which are still in basic production today. Among these are the Models 1891 and 1893 (today designated Models 39 and 336). These were shoulder arms that were popular with exhibition shooters such as Annie Oakley.

After their father's death in 1901, two of Marlin's sons took over his business and expanded the product line. In 1915, the company was bought by a group of New York investors and renamed the Marlin-Rickwell Corporation; it soon became one of the world's largest manufacturers of machine guns for United States and Allied troops in World War I.

In 1924, the company was offered at auction and purchased by a lawyer, Frank Kenna. Kenna continued producing many of the popular models and added a division making razor blades.

In 1953, Marlin Firearms patented and began producing firearms with a new technique, MicroGroove Rifling. This process was conceived to increase the speed by which barrels could be manufactured.

The Kenna family operated the company until its sale to the Remington Arms Company in 2007.

Golden 60SN Scoped

Golden 39A

60C

60S-CF

60SB

70PSS Stainless

308 Marlin Express

Marlin

308MXLR
with Scope

336C

336SS

336XLR

338MX

336W with Scope

338MXLR

915YS

795

917

917VS

1895

Mossberg

In 1919, Oscar Frederick Mossberg along with his sons, Iver and Harold, established O. F. Mossberg & Sons, Inc. The company initially produced a .22 caliber handgun nicknamed the "Brownie." There followed, in quick succession, Brownie .22 caliber rifles, shotguns, and rifle scopes. The product line was increasingly diversified to include golf clubs, gun racks, campers, and sailboats.

Over the years, the company continued to develop innovative new products and techniques: Monte Carlo-type stocks, molded trigger housings, and spring-loaded, quick-release swivels. O. F. Mossberg & Sons, Inc, is not only the oldest family controlled firearms manufacturer in the United States but also the world's largest producer of pump-action shotguns.

Still under family control today, the company manufactures popular and industry-standard firearms for home security, personal protection, military, and law enforcement uses.

464™ Lever-Action Rifle

4x4 Bolt-Action Centerfire
Walnut Stock

4x4 Bolt-Action Centerfire
Black Skeletonized Block

4x4 Bolt-Action
Scoped Combo

4x4 Bolt-Action
Laminate Stock

MMR™ Hunter 5.56mm NATO (.223 Rem)

MVP Varmint 24" Scoped

100 ATR Short-Action Walnut

100 ATR Long-Action Black Synthetic

100 ATR Scoped Combo Black Synthetic

Mossberg

464 Lever-Action Wood Stock

702 Bantam Plinkster

702 Bantam Plinkster Scoped Combo

18″ 702 Plinkster Thumbhole Tipdown

22″ 702 Plinkster Thumbhole Tipdown

22″ 702 Plinkster Thumbhole Tipdown Wood

801 Half-Pint Plinkster

802 Plinkster Black Synthetic

817 Bolt-Action Black Synthetic

817 Thumbhole Tipdown Black Synthetic

817 Bolt-Action Wood Stock

817 Varmint Black Synthetic

Pedersoli

Founded in 1957, the Davide Pedersoli & C. began with the manufacture of hunting shotguns, under-and-over shotguns, and side-by-side shotguns. By 1960, the company had added a line of muzzle-loading guns, which by the early 1970s became its major product. In fact, by 1973 no more traditional hunting shotguns were being produced by the firm. The whole concentration of the company was focused on the manufacture of historical muzzle-loading guns and their accessories, including powder flasks.

In 1982, to further ensure production standards, the company began the manufacture of all of the wooden and metal components for the muzzle-loading guns. Therefore the muzzle-loading and breech-loading guns could be completely produced and finished in-house. As the demand for accessories grew, a new allied company was started up, Universal Special Accessories Company (U.S.A.), for their production and distribution.

Today the company still remains in family hands, run by Davide's son, Pierangelo Pedersoli, and his brother-in-law, Giovanni Gottardi.

High-Wall Sporting

1874 Sharps Old West "Maple"

1874 Sharps Old West "Walnut"

High Wall Sporting .38 Winchester

High-Wall Sporting

Mississippi Rolling Block Sporting

High-Wall Classic

Remington

According to legend, in 1816 Eliphalet Remington II believed he could build a better gun than he could buy, and so he set out to do just that. Even though he came in second in a shooting competition with his homemade flintlock rifle, other contestants wanted to buy it. In 1828, his gun business had outgrown his workshop in his hometown of Ilion Gorge, New York. He started a new facility in Ilion, close to the recently opened Erie Canal. The site of that early facility is still home to a Remington arms factory today.

The Remington Company was responsible for the design and implementation of the first hammerless solid-breech repeating shotgun, and hammerless auto-loading shotgun. They also manufactured the first successful high-power slide-action repeating rifle and lock-breech auto-loading rifle. As business continued to grow, in 1865 Remington incorporated and took on stockholders. In 1873, he expanded his product line and began manufacturing typewriters. Eventually the company split into Remington Rand, later Sperry Rand (which produced the typewriters), and the Remington Arms Company. Remington sold the typewriter business in 1886.

Marcus Hartley and Partners, a large sporting goods firm bought Remington Arms in 1888 and opened a second facility in Bridgeport, Connecticut. In 1912, Remington merged with another Hartley company, Union Metallic Cartridge to form Remington UMC.

During World War I, Remington increased manufacturing facilities, and after the war, to take full advantage of these new capabilities, Remington began making pocket and hunting knives, household utensils, and cash registers. They created a cloth patch with their logo for marketing purposes, and this eventually developed into yet another product line, clothing.

Prior to World War II, Remington worked in collaboration with the United States government to expand ammunition and arms production. In 1940, Remington was asked to construct new production plants in Salt Lake City, Utah; Denver, Colorado; Lake City, Minnesota; King Mills, Ohio; and Lowell, Massachusetts. Although the plants were owned by the government, they were operated by Remington.

Until the present day, Remington continues to bring out innovative lines of rifles and shotguns, ammunition, accessories, and clay pigeons, and to expand their production facilities throughout the country.

700 BDL

700 CDL

40XB KS

40XB Tactical

40-XB Rangemaster Thumbhole Stock

The Model 700 CDLTM 375 H&H 100th Anniversary Rifle

597

504-T LS HB

572 BDL
Smoothbore

597 VTR

597 Blaze Camo

597 Pink Camo

597 TVP

700 Varmint SF

700 VTR
Desert Recon

700 Target
Tactical

Remington

700 XCR REMO Edition

700 CDL SF

R-15 VTR Predator Thumbhole

R-15 VTR Predator
SS Varmint

R-15 VTR Predator
Byson South Edition

R-25 308 Winchester

Rossi

Amadeo Rossi established the Rossi Company in 1889. The founder's goal was to produce an affordable product without giving up an accuracy or quality in Sao Paolo, Brazil.

In 1997, in order to better control their sales, Rossi set up BrazTech International as an exclusive importer of Rossi products in North America.

Rossi is known for the production of revolvers, single-shot rifles, muzzleloaders, and lever-action rifles. In 2003 Rossi was honored with the awards of "Best of the Best" and "Best Value" from *Field & Stream* magazine for its Rossi Trifecta. The versatile Trifecta is like three guns in one, as the system includes barrels for a .243 Winchester, 22 Long Rifle, and a 20-gauge shotgun.

Rossi is still in the hands of the original family.

Rio Grande Lever-Action .410 guage

Circuit Judge Lever Action

M92 .44 Blue 12+1 24" Oct Barrel

M92 .38/357 Blue 12+1 24" Oct Barrel

M92 .38/357 Blue/ Case Hdnd 12+1 24" Oct Barrel

M92 Carbine .38/357 Blue 8+1 16" Large Loop

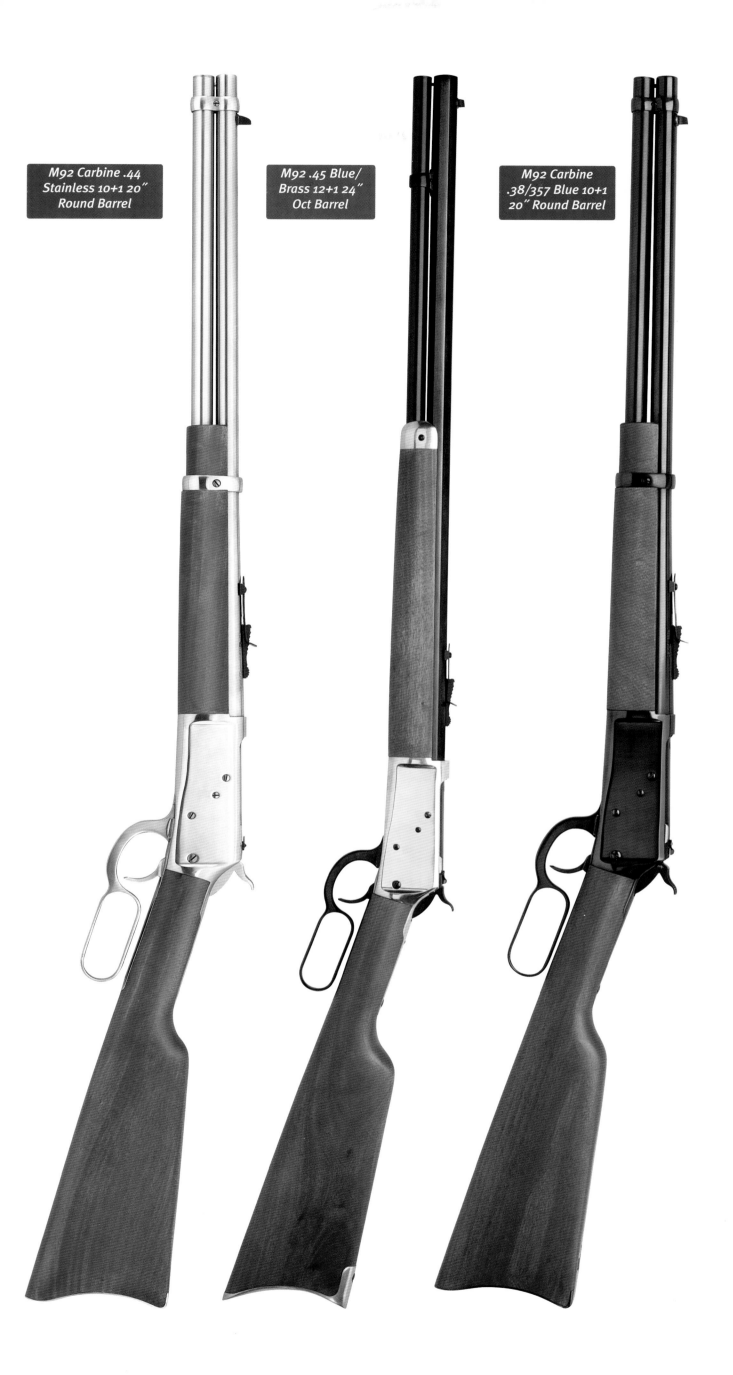

M92 Carbine .44 Stainless 10+1 20″ Round Barrel

M92 .45 Blue/ Brass 12+1 24″ Oct Barrel

M92 Carbine .38/357 Blue 10+1 20″ Round Barrel

Rossi

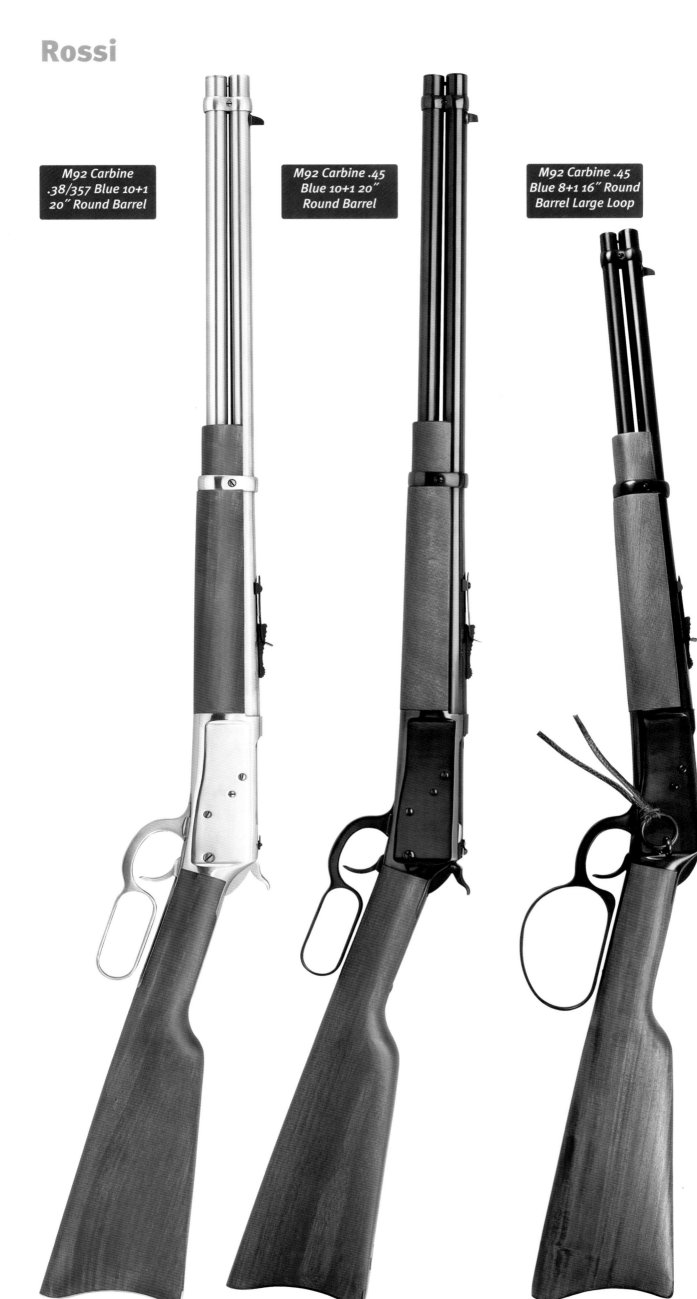

M92 Carbine
.38/357 Blue 10+1
20" Round Barrel

M92 Carbine .45
Blue 10+1 20"
Round Barrel

M92 Carbine .45
Blue 8+1 16" Round
Barrel Large Loop

*M92 Rifle .44
Blue/Case Hdnd
10+1 20˝ Oct Barrel*

*M92 Carbine .44
Stainless 10+1 20˝
Round Barrel*

*M92 Carbine .44
Blue 10+1 20˝
Round Barrel With
Ring and Scope
Mount*

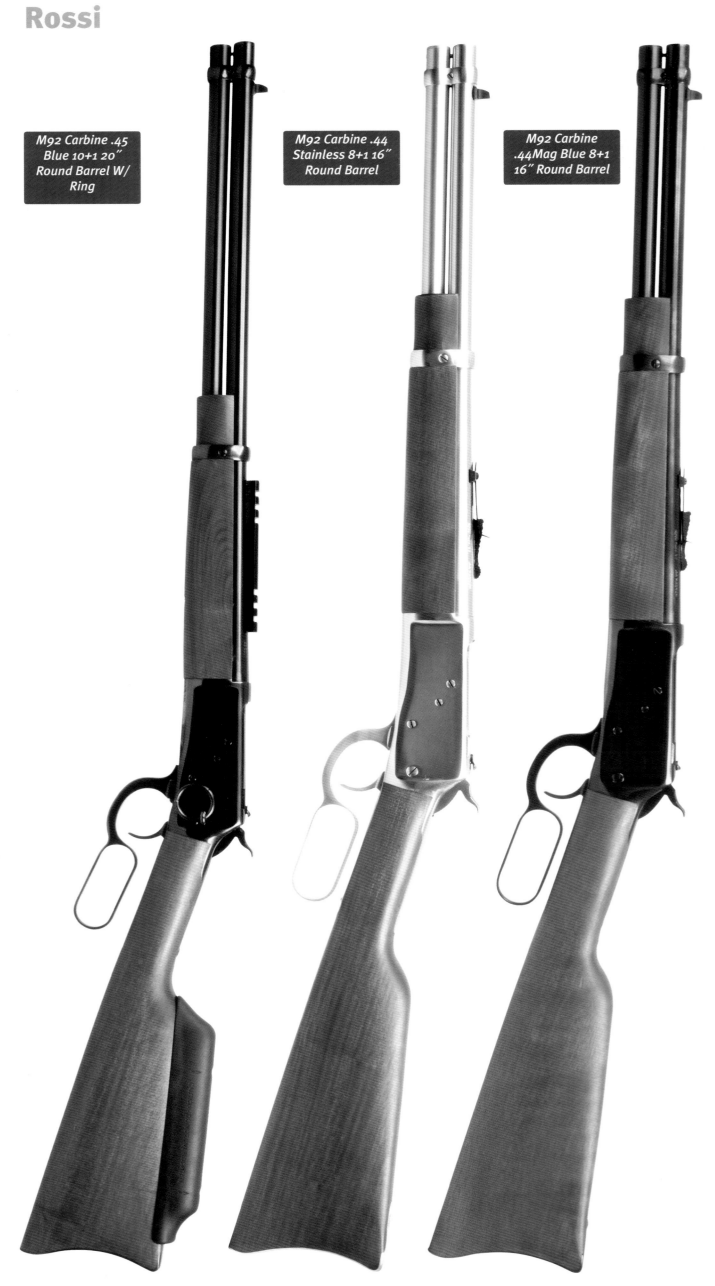

M92 Carbine .45
Blue 10+1 20"
Round Barrel W/
Ring

M92 Carbine .44
Stainless 8+1 16"
Round Barrel

M92 Carbine
.44Mag Blue 8+1
16" Round Barrel

Full-Size .223
Single-Shot Rifle

Youth Size .243
Single-Shot Rifle

Full-Size .308
Single-Shot Rifle

Ruger

Ruger (the common name for Sturm, Ruger & Co,) is the largest maker of firearms in the United States, as well as one of the few to make all three major lines of firearms: handguns, shotguns, and rifles. Their corporate motto is, "Arms Makers for Responsible Citizens."

Founded by William B. Ruger and Alexander McCormick Sturm in 1949 in a small rented machine shop in Southport, Connecticut, it first produced a well-received 22-caliber pistol. Some of the design features of the pistol came out of Ruger's earlier work studying and adapting techniques from two Baby Nambu pistols he had received from a United States Marine who had brought them home from Japan after World War II. Although the company decided not to market the actual pistols, they did use the Nambu's rear-style cocking device and silhouette in the concept for the .22-caliber pistols.

Ruger has been an important manufacturer of the .22-rimfire rifle with their popular Ruger 10/22. Sales can be credited to its relative low cost and good quality combined with a large number of accessories and available parts. Ruger also has a large share of the .22-rimfire semiautomatic pistol market.

In 1951 Alex Sturm died, and the company continued to be run by William B. Ruger until his death in 2002. Since 1969, Sturm, Ruger has been a public company and, in 1990, became a New York Stock Exchange company.

Between 1949 and 2004, Ruger produced and marketed more than twenty million firearms. Today, Ruger manufactures and distributes a wide range of firearms for use in hunting, target shooting, self-defense, collecting, and law enforcement.

SR 556

M77 Gunsite Scout Rifle

10/22 Compact Autoloading Rifle

10/22 Target Autoloading Rifle

10/22 Target Autoloading Rifle Stainless

10/22 Carbine Autoloading Rifle Black Synthetic Stainless

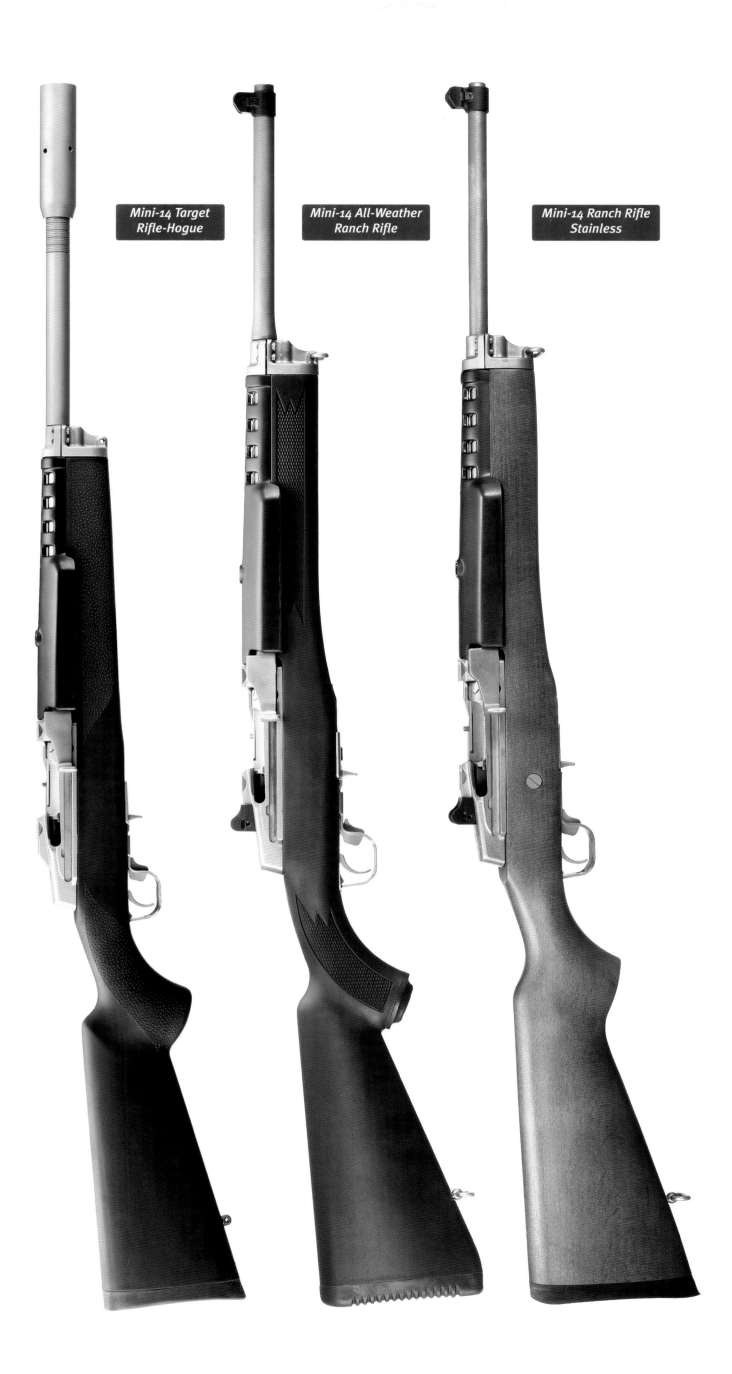

Mini-14 Target Rifle-Hogue

Mini-14 All-Weather Ranch Rifle

Mini-14 Ranch Rifle Stainless

Ruger

Mini-14 Target Ranch
Rifle Laminate

Mini-14 Rifle
With ATI Stock

Mini-14
Tactical Rifle

Mini-14 Ranch
Rifle Alloy Steel

SR-556
Autoloading Rifle

M77 Hawkeye
All-Weather Rifle

M77 Compact
Magnum Rifle
American Walnut

M77 Mark II
Target Rifle

77/22 Rotary
Magazine Rifle

No.1 Varminter
Single-Shot Rifle

No.1 Medium
Sporter
Single-Shot Rifle

Sako

Located in Riihimäki, Finland, Sako Limited (Suojeluskuntain Ase- ja Konepaja Oy, Civil Guard Gun- and Machiningworks Ltd) was established in June, 1927, from the Suojeluskuntain Yliesikunnan Asepaja (Civil Guard Supreme Staff Gun Works). Sako originally was conceived to design and make firearms for the Finnish Civil Guard. During World War II, Sako firearms had an important role in Finland's struggle against the Nazis.

For many decades, Sako solely developed and manufactured military arms, target and hunting rifles, and cartridges. Despite several shifts in organization, Sako remained a privately held firm and is now associated with Beretta Holdings. In recent decades, Sako has continued to produce civilian rifles for hunting, while still producing several lines for military and security purposes.

85 Varmint Laminated Stainless

85 Hunter

85 Bavarian

85 Classic

85 Deluxe

85 Finnlight

85 Hunter Laminate
Stainless

85 Kodiak

85 Safari

Sako

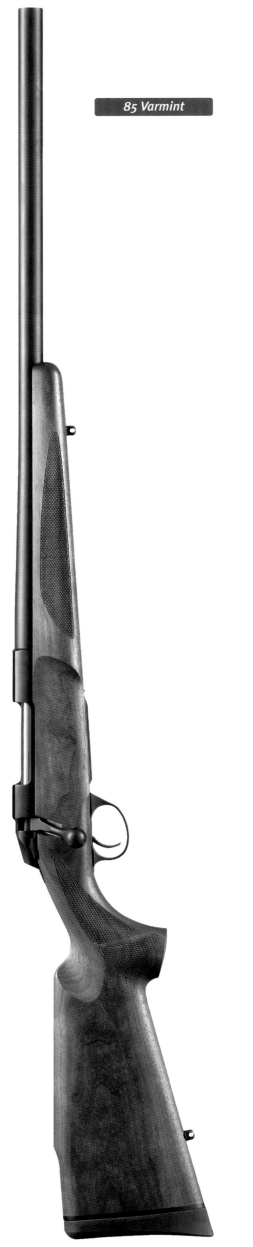

85 Varmint

85 Synthetic Stainless

Quad Heavy Barrel

Quad Hunter Pro

Quad Synthetic

Quad Varmint

SIG Sauer

The beginnings of the SIG Sauer firm began more than 150 years ago in 1853 in Rhone Falls, Switzerland, when Friedrich Peyer im Hof, Heinrich Moser, and Conrad Neher opened a wagon factory in the small town. They built one of the most modern factories of its day devoted to building wagons and railroad cars. After just seven years, they entered into a competition to develop a modern rifle for the Swiss Army. They won a contract from the army for 30,000 muzzle-loading Prelaz-Burnand rifles and promptly changed the company name to the Swiss Industrial Company: Schweizerische Industrie-Gesellschaft, known as SIG.

Up until the beginning of World War II, Sauer mainly manufactured shotguns and hunting rifles. During the war, they produced the Sauer 38H, a small automatic pistol.

In the 1970s, SIG wanted to work on a pistol that would balance cost with quality. By Swiss law, there are limits on the ability of Swiss companies to manufacture firearms, mandating that a Swiss company must partner with a foreign firm. SIG chose to join with the German firm of Sauer & Sohn, and the SIG Sauer series of handguns began with the SIG Sauer

SIG P220 handgun in 1975. Up until the beginning of World War II, Sauer mainly manufactured shotguns and hunting rifles. During the war, they produced the Sauer 38H, a small automatic pistol.

The year 1985 saw the creation of SIGARMS, the American branch of SIG in Tysons Corner, Virginia. The divisions was established in order to import the P220 and P230 semiautomatic handguns. In 1987, SIGARMS moved to Herndon, Virginia, and then to Exeter, New Hampshire, in 1990.

In October of 2002, Michael Lüke and Thomas Ortmeier took over SIGARMS, and its European sister companies, Sauer & Sohn, Blaser, Mauser, and Swiss Arms. SIG Sauer, the largest of the five companies, is one of the major firearms producers in the world. As far as its growth in the United States, it has expanded sales more than fifty percent since 2005.

SIGARMS changed its name officially to SIG Sauer in October 2007. Most recently, the U.S. Coast Guard awarded SIG Sauer a contract to produce their standard issue firearm, and the Office of Homeland Security and Customs Enforcement also has selected them as one of their exclusive suppliers.

552

SIG 50

556 with Bipod

P516 10"

Blaser LRS2

SSG 3000

Smith & Wesson

In 1852 two New Englanders, Horace Smith and Dan Wesson, joined forces to found the Smith & Wesson Company. Smith had learned about firearms while working at the National Armory in Springfield, Massachusetts. Wesson's experience was gleaned from his years as an apprentice to his brother, Edwin, a famous maker of target pistols and rifles. They opened a facility in Norwich, Connecticut, to design and produce lever–action repeating pistols with fully self-contained cartridges. This did not prove to be a success, and in 1854 they sold the company to a shirt manufacturer, Oliver Winchester, who went on (in 1866) to use their design as the basis for his Winchester Repeating Arms Company.

The two men tried again in 1856, forming a partnership to produce a revolver to fire the rimfire cartridge. This became the earliest fully self-contained revolver available in the world. Smith & Wesson held the patents which prevented others from producing similar firearms.

Their next design was ready for market in 1870—the Model 3 American, the first large-caliber cartridge revolver. They also gained two major new clients for the .357 weapon: the United States Cavalry and the Russian Imperial Army.

Toward the end of the century, Smith retired, selling his shares in the firm to Wesson. The company soon introduced a line of hammerless revolvers that are still produced today.

Possibly the most famous contribution of Smith & Wesson was the .38 Military & Police or the Model 10. In continual production since its inception, the Model 10 is used by nearly every police and military force in existence.

In 1935 Smith & Wesson continued to add both to their product line and their worldwide reputation with the development and manufacture of the first Magnum revolver, the .375. Later, in 1955, they followed with the production of the Model 39.

Perhaps the most well-known Magnum in the line was introduced in 1956—the .44 Magnum used by Clint Eastwood in his movie role as *Dirty Harry*. The first stainless steel Magnum, Model 60, was first produced in 1965.

Today, in addition to its lengthy register of renowned firearms, the Smith & Wesson brand produces bicycles, gun accessories, handcuffs, safes, clothing, collectibles, knives, tools, air guns, cologne, and handbags among many other items.

M&P 15 Sport

M&P 15-22 (Standard)

M&P 15 5.56 mm

M&P 15T

M&P 15

M&P15 MOE Mid MAGPUL® SPEC SERIES™

i-Bolt Black

i-Bolt Camo

i-Bolt Weathershield
Black

M&P 15-22 Rifle
(Compliant)

M&P 15A

i-Bolt Weathershield Camo

Springfield Armory

Established in 1794 in Springfield, Massachusetts, Springfield Armory was opened under the authority of George Washington during the Revolutionary War. It became the first U.S. National Armory and was used for the manufacturing, testing, storage, repair, and development of military small arms, including muskets and rifles. Despite being a pioneer of firearms and firearm manufacturing methods, Springfield Armory was closed in 1968 after 174 years of U.S. government service.

The legendary name "Springfield Armory" was trademarked by Elmer C. Balance, owner of LH Manufacturing in San Antonio, Texas. Forefronting the company's success in 1974 was the production of the first civilian M14 rifle, the M1A rifle. However, amidst its increasing popularity, Balance sold Springfield Armory to Robert Reese, a man with a well-established production shop and firearms experience. Reese expanded the company's market with the production of the notable M1911 pistol.

The Springfield Armory Company, now located in Geneseo, Illinois, is run by Robert Reese's two sons Dennis and Tom. They continued to gain success by branching into many other fields of firearms, offering clones of M1 Garand rifles, Beretta BM59, FN FAL, HK 91, and AR-15, also importing Tanfoglio and Astra semiautomatic pistols under the Springfield name. However, the company's main products still remain the M1911 pistol (built using Brazilian components produced by IMBEL) and the M1A semiautomatic rifle series.

Springfield Armory also has a well-known custom shop headed by gunsmith David Williams, with well known previous directors including Les Baer and Jack Weigand. Full-custom M1911A1s and semicustom XD pistols are built and modified here, as well as their most famous product, the Tactical Response Pistol Professional Model (formerly known as the Bureau Model). The TRP Professional was one of only two guns to pass the controversial trials set forth by the Federal Bureau of Investigation for a new pistol for its Hostage Rescue Team and SWAT teams.

Today the Springfield Armory proudly bares the motto "the first name in American firearms," a reference to its historical name trademarked from the original Springfield Armory in Springfield, Massachusetts.

Among the company's noted accomplishments is also the inception of the practical shooting team in 1985, where Rob Leatham is captain of Team Springfield.

MA9226 M1A

AA9628 M1A Socom II Camo

AA9626 Socom 16

AA9616 Scout Squad Black Composite

MA9106 M1A
Standard Black
Composite Stock

MA9826 M1A
Loaded Black Com-
posite Stock

NA9102 M1A
National Match
Walnut Match

Steyr Mannlicher

According to legend, the city of Steyr, Austria, has been involved with firearms production since the 1400s. It was in April, 1864, that Josef Werndl founded the "Josef und Franz Werndl & Comp. Waffenfabrik und Sägemühle in Oberletten" (Josef and Franz Werndl & Partners Weapons Factory and Sawmill in Oberletten). Somewhat later, this became "Österreichische Waffenfabriksgesellschaft" (OEWG, Austrian Arms-Manufacturing Company), and finally came to be the Steyr Werke AG and Steyr-Daimler-Puch AG. Steyr Mannlicher was a part of this final firm.

By the beginning of World War I, the company employed more than 15,000 workers and manufactured more than 4,000 guns per day. After the end of the war, production of arms in the town of Steyr was all but forbidden and the company faced financial disaster.

In order to survive those difficult times, the company converted their equipment to the production of automobiles. It was not until the onset of World War II that the firm began to produce firearms once again.

The Mannlicher-Schönauer full-stock rifle was popular once more in part due to the reestablishment of the Austrian Armed Forces. In the 1970s, Steyr was able to commence a new line of military weapons design including a new assault-type rifle, the StG 77. It was built from all synthetic materials and had an integrated fixed optic system.

Today, Steyr produces firearms in several classes for use in hunting, by the military, and for sportsmen.

Big Bore

Big Bore Camo

Classic Mountain

Classic Halfstock

Classic Fullstock

Classic Light

Luxus Standard

Luxus with Engraved Sideplates

Steyr Mannlicher

Pro African

Pro Alaskan

Pro Hunter Mountain

Pro Hunter
Camouflage

Pro Hunter
Timber

Pro Hunter
Stainless

Steyr Mannlicher

Pro Varmint

Pro Varmint Camouflage

Pro Varmint with Optic

Scout

Scout With Imitated Wood Inserts

Elite

Steyr Mannlicher

Elite 08

SSG 04

SSG 08 Camo

SSG 69 PII

AUG A3

Thompson/Center

Thompson/Center Arms Company was set up in 1965 when a convenient colloboration between K. W. Thompson Tool Company, which was seeking new products to fill its production capabilities, partnered with Warren Center, a gun designer in search of a manufacturer for his Contender pistol. Thompson Tool's facilities were expanded and the new company Thompson/Center, was formed in Rochester, New Hampshire. It took only two years for the first Contender pistols to ship, and the company has been producing hunting handguns ever since. Today, Thompson/Center has marketed more than 400,000 of these pistols.

Two years later, the first Contender pistol was shipped, starting a trend in high-performance hunting handguns, which continues to grow every year.

To date, over 400,000 Contender pistols have been shipped and the pistol's reputation for versatility, accuracy, and dependability goes unchallenged among serious handgun shooters.

The company became known for its line of interchangeable barrel single-shot pistols and rifles. The company has also helped spur a resurgance of interest in muzzle-loading rifles, which they began manufacturing in 1970 with the introduction of the Hawken Muzzleloading rifle.

In the present day, Thompson/Center's product line includes single-shot pistols and rifles, and a full line of muzzleloading rifles and accessories. The original version of the Contender pistol has been updated as the G2 Contender and is one of the best-known hunting handguns available today.

Encore® Pro Hunter™ XT muzzleloader

IMPACT™ muzzleloader

Icon 30TC With Scope

Icon Classic Walnut

Icon Precision Hunter With Scope

Icon Weather Shield

Dimension Rifle

Thompson/Center

R-55 All Weather Composite

R-55 Benchmark

R-55 Classic

Venture With Scope

Triumph With Scope

Triumph Camouflage
With Scope

Uberti

A. Uberti, S.r.l. was established in 1959 by Aldo Uberti in the Italian Alps foothill village of Gardone Val Trompia. The company is a daughter to the well-known Beretta firearms company and resides within the Beretta industrial complex.

Dedicated to creating high-quality replicas, Uberti took his first project in 1959 reproducing the 1851 Navy Colt in commemoration of the hundredth anniversary of the American Civil War, positively establishing the company's reputation. The continued popularity of their reproductions led to the manufacturing of the 1866 Winchester lever-action replica in 1965, as well as the Colt Single-Action Army replica called "Cattleman" in 1966.

Movie directors began consulting Aldo Uberti to reproduce guns for Western films. In 1960, well-known Italian movie director Sergio Leone was the first to use Uberti Old West replicas in his series of Western films, which later would come to be known as "spaghetti Westerns." These movie sets, featuring characters clad with Uberti replica firearms, sparked an international fascination with Italian-made guns. Among the Western films contributing to the Uberti replica notoriety are popular films such as *The Outlaw Josey Wales*, *A Fistful of Dollars* trilogy, *Dances with Wolves*, and *Tombstone*.

Uberti is currently the world's largest reproducer of historical American firearms, manufacturing about 30,000 handguns and 10,000 rifles annually. They employ about sixty skilled artisans to fit and assemble the precisely cast and cut parts as they come off the computer numerical control machinery. With the fast-growing Civil War and Western reenactment industry, Uberti replica firearms have become a staple to the gun-manufacturing industry.

1874 Cavalry Carbine Sharps

1874 Sharps Hunter

1873 Carbine

1874 "Long Range" Sharps

Baby Rolling Block Carbine

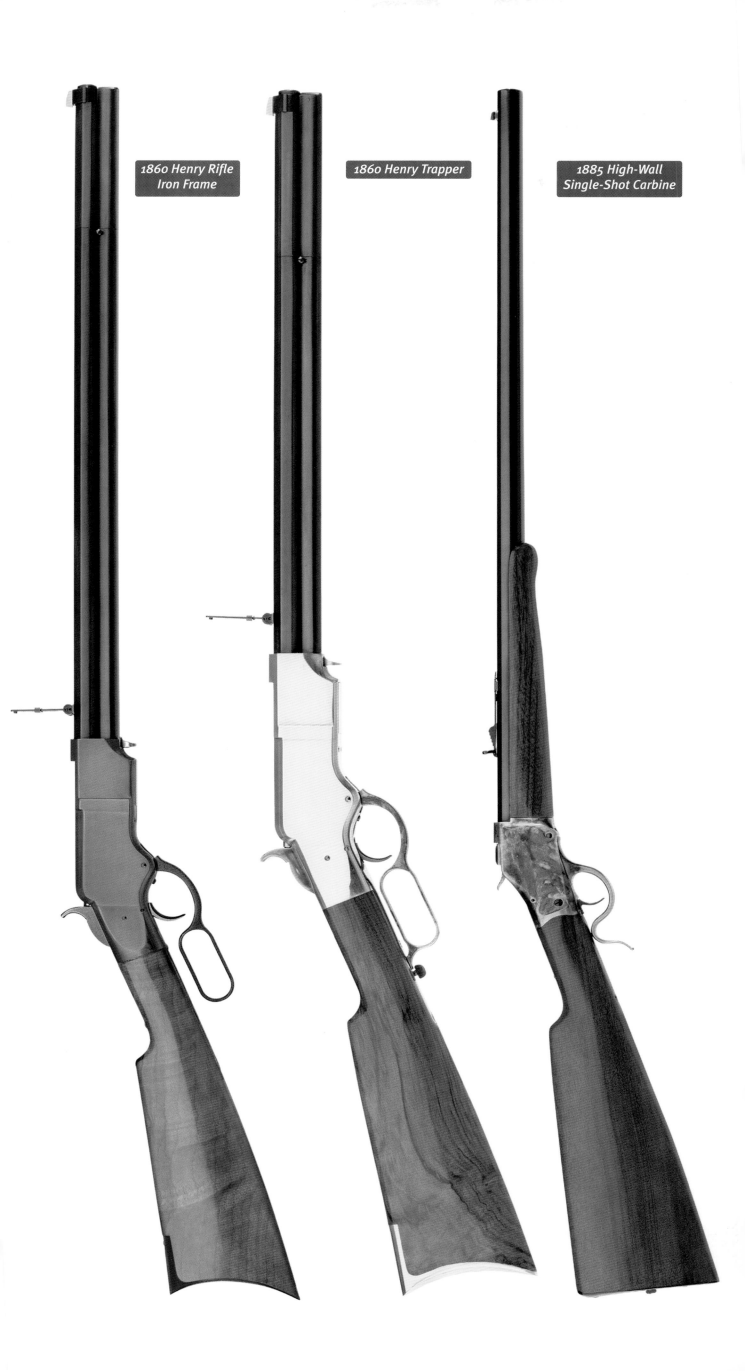

1860 Henry Rifle Iron Frame

1860 Henry Trapper

1885 High-Wall Single-Shot Carbine

Walther

In 1886 Carl Walther opened his first production facility for Walther Works in Zella-Mehlis, Thuringia, in Germany, an area famous for its gunmakers. In 1908 Walther's concept was to build a self-loading handgun; he marketed the first German self-loading Walther Model 1, caliber 6.35 mm. In World War I, almost every German soldier was issued a Walther pocket gun.

Carl Walther died in 1915, and was succeeded in the business by his son Fritz who kept honing the self-loading technology. In 1929 Fritz made the first single-/double-action trigger pistol, the Walther Model PP. This was soon followed by a compact model PPK. In 1938, at the request of the German military, Walther developed a more powerful version with the 9 mm cartridge in the Model P38. The classic design of this gun is still used today and imitated by many firearms makers.

During World War II, the Walther factory was destroyed. Fritz managed to salvage some of the design plans, however, and brought them with him to West Germany after the end of the war. By 1953 he had completed building a new factory in the city of Ulm along the banks of the Danube in Germany. The main Walther factory is still there today.

In 1993 Walther merged with Umarex and expanded their reach on a more global basis. Together they have produced the Model 99, nicknamed "the First Pistol of the Next Century," which is mainly used by police and military forces. In the 1996 Summer Olympics in Atlanta, Georgia, Walther pistols were used by some of the gold medalists.

G22 A1 Black

G22 A2 Black

G22 A3 Black

G22 Black

G22 Military

Weatherby

In 1945, Roy Weatherby set up his arms company in order to produce guns to his concept that lightweight bullets moving at very fast speeds were the best for one-shot kills. He spent the next ten years perfecting high-powered Weatherby Magnum cartridges. The company is still known for these cartridges. He also designed and produced rifles that were specifically equipped to handle his new type of ammunition.

In 1957, he developed a new gun, the Mark V, which was a stronger, safer weapon able to stand up to great pressure. Then again in 1970, he conceived another innovative product the Weatherby Vanguard, with many of the traits of the Mark V but with two locking lugs.

In 1983, Weatherby's son, Ed, took over the company and has overseen the expansion of the Mark V and Vanguard lines of weapons as well as adding semiautomatic, pump, side-by-side, and over/under shotguns. All support lines of accompanying accessories, in addition to a line of apparel and collectibles.

Mark V Lapua TRR

Mark V Accumark

Mark V Royal

Mark V Deluxe

Mark V Safari

Mark V Fibermark

Mark V Lazermark

Mark V Sporter

Mark V Synthetic

Mark V Ultramark

Weatherby

Vanguard Carbine

Vanguard Predator

Vanguard Sporter

Vanguard Sub Moa

Vanguard Sub Moa Varmint

Mark XXII

Winchester

In 1855, Horace Smith and Dan Wesson established Volcanic Repeating Arms Company in Norwich, Connecticut, in order to produce their Volcanic lever-action rifle. In 1856, the company was renamed the New Haven Arms company and moved to that city. The Volcanic rifle used Hunt's Rocket Ball ammunition and did not meet with any great commercial success. Eventually B. T. Henry redesigned the gun to allow it to use different ammunition, and it became known as the Henry rifle. In 1862, the first Henry rifles were sold and used in large numbers by the Union forces during the Civil War.

In 1866, Oliver Winchester bought control of New Haven Arms Company and changed its name to Winchester Repeating Arms Company. The first gun to have the Winchester name was the Model 1866 Yellow Boy lever action.

In the 1880s, John Browning collaborated with the Winchester firm to formulate and build a series of repeating rifles and shotguns that included the Winchester Model 1885 Single-Shot, Winchester Model 1887 lever-action shotgun, Model 1897 pump-action shotgun, and Model 1895 (with a box magazine) rifle.

By the beginning of the twentieth century, however, Winchester Repeating Arms was actually in competition with new John Browning designs manufactured by several other companies.

There was heated competition during this period to devise the first commercially viable self-loading rifle. Winchester produced the .22 rimfire Winchester Model 1903, as well as several later models.

In 1911, Winchester brought out its first semi-automatic shotgun, which was followed in the next year by a pump-action shotgun. The first bolt-action rifle was introduced in 1919. Yet another first was the 1930 production of a side-by-side.

With the advent of World War I, the company was a main supplier of the Enfield rifles to both the United States and British governments. Unfortunately, heavy borrowing during the war to support the necessary increase in production capabilities left the company nearly bankrupt, and in 1931, Winchester Repeating Arms was purchased by Olin Industries.

In World War II, they produced the M1 Garand rifle and later manufactured the M14 rifle.

The rest of the 20th century was a time of financial upheaval for the firm. At the beginning of 2006, U.S. Repeating Arms, as Winchester had been renamed, announced the closing of the New Haven plant where the first Winchester arms had been produced more than 140 years earlier. Later that same year, Olin Industries stated that the Winchester product line would be built by Browning, a subsidiary of FN Herstal.

Model 70 Coyote Light

Wildcat Bolt-Action 22

Wildcat Target/Varmint

Model 1895, Grade I

Model 71 Deluxe

Theodore Roosevelt
150th Model 1895
Custom Grade

Model 1895 Safari
Centennial High
Grade

Model 1895 Safari
Centennial Custom
Grade

Winchester

Model 70 Super Grade

Model 70 Sporter

Model 70 Featherweight

Model 70 Extreme Weather SS

Model 70 Ultimate Shadow

Model 70 Safari Express

Index

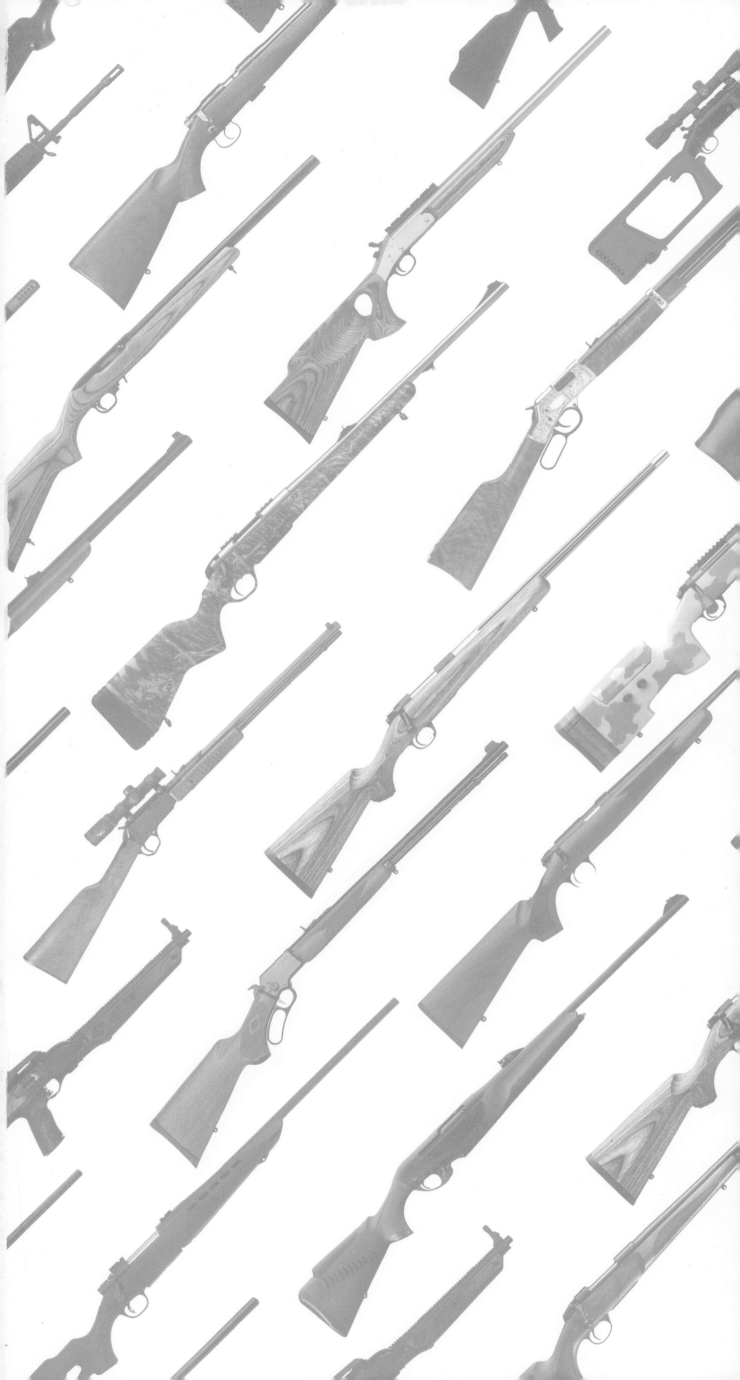